EXECUTION

A HISTORY OF CAPITAL PUNISHMENT IN BRITAIN

EXECUTION

A HISTORY OF CAPITAL PUNISHMENT IN BRITAIN

SIMON WEBB

First published 2011

The History Press
The Mill, Brimscombe Port
Stroud, Gloucestershire, GL5 2QG
www.thehistorypress.co.uk

Reprinted 2017

British Library Cataloguing in Publication Data.
A catalogue record for this book is available from the British Library.

ISBN 978 0 7524 6407 7

Typesetting and origination by The History Press

CONTENTS

INTRODUCTION

It is a sobering thought that for all but the last twelve or fifteen years Britain's courts have been able to impose the death penalty for a variety of offences; both military and civil. Although the last murderers were hanged in 1964, death remained the punishment for a number of crimes, ranging from arson in Royal Dockyards and piracy on the high seas to treason, espionage and inciting mutiny in the army during time of war. It was not until a few months before the end of the twentieth century that the death penalty was finally abolished in this country for all offences. Even beheading was only removed from the statute book as recently as 1973.

This book is an account of capital punishment in Britain from the Roman occupation up to the present day. It charts the rise, decline and final abandonment of a practice which many other countries today have also rejected; that of killing those who transgress against the laws of the land, rather than fining or imprisoning them. It is almost fifty years since the last execution in this country and despite occasional demands for the return of capital punishment, usually following some particularly disgusting murder by terrorists or child abusers; the majority of us seem content that the grisly ritual of execution should remain a historical curiosity.

Most people, if asked about executions in this country, will think at once of hanging. This is perhaps inevitable; nobody has been put to death in this country by any other method since the shooting of two men at Shepton Mallet Prison in Somerset in 1944. Hanging is all that most of us can recall.

However, a variety of other methods for killing criminals have been used in this country over the centuries. These range from beheading with the axe and block, to boiling in a cauldron and crushing to death. It is worth asking ourselves at this juncture what the point was of executing people in such dreadful ways as burning them alive or cutting out their hearts? The answer is simple enough, although based upon a massive misunderstanding of human nature.

It was believed, at one time, that if the penalties for committing a crime were made harsh enough, then people would be discouraged from committing them in the first place. They would see the awful consequences for the perpetrators who were caught and punished, and the result would be a reduction in the rate of this particular offence. However, we will see that when the so-called, 'Bloody Code' was in force and death was the penalty for over 200 offences, crimes were still committed with reckless abandon. Indeed, the crowds which gathered to watch the executions at Tyburn were generally acknowledged to be full of thieves and pickpockets, who took the opportunity presented by public executions to ply their trade, running the risk of being hanged themselves if detected in the act of theft.

It is not frightful punishments which deter crime, but the likelihood of detection. As long as the chances of being caught are slight, people will risk committing a crime. If one is likely to be caught, then even if the penalty faced is only a year or two in prison, rates for this particular crime will fall. It was not the Bloody Code which reduced crime in Britain, but rather the creation of an efficient police force.

Despite the fact that hanging was by far-and-away the most common method of capital punishment used in Britain, there is no record of its use before the coming of the Anglo-Saxons in the fifth century AD. The first named victims of capital punishment, recorded in this country, died not by the rope but by having their heads struck off with swords. It seems appropriate then to begin our investigation of executions in this country with decapitation.

All illustrations are from the author's collection unless stated otherwise.

Simon Webb, 2011

BEHEADING BY SWORD, AXE AND ROPE

Britain has a very ancient tradition of decapitation (as beheading is more technically known). The Celts, who inhabited these islands before the Roman invasion, were enthusiastic head-hunters, who collected and preserved human heads as trophies. According to some classical writers, they pickled these grisly souvenirs in cedar oil and passed them round to be admired during banquets. Almost invariably though, the severing of these heads from their bodies took place after death. The subjects of such mutilations were enemies slain in battle, rather than convicted criminals. The first recorded judicial execution by beheading, in this country, did not take place until the end of the third century AD, during the Roman occupation.

The Romans regarded death by beheading as the only honourable form of execution. It was the most dignified, and least painful, mode of capital punishment used in the Roman Empire. This was a death which was associated with the nobility; it was seldom inflicted upon common criminals. Both Mark Anthony's grandfather and also his son were executed in this way, as were a number of famous statesmen such as Cicero. These decapitations were achieved by using a sword rather than an axe.

Before we go any further, it is perhaps worth mentioning that executions by beheading are unusual in that they typically require a good deal of cooperation from the victim if they are to be carried out successfully. The condemned person must remain perfectly still and not move, flinch or even distract the headsman at any time. Even so, accidents and miscalculations can occur and the consequences can be horrific. An example from France illustrates this point perfectly.

In 1699, Angelique Ticquet arranged to have her husband murdered. This resulted in her being sentenced to death; the execution to take place by beheading with a sword in public. On the day of the execution, a thunderstorm broke just as Ticquet was about to ascend the scaffold. She then had the thoroughly unnerving experience of having to shelter from the rain with Charles Sanson, the public executioner who was to remove her head. Sanson did not wish to risk carrying out an execution while it was raining. The heavy, double-handed sword required considerable dexterity to wield effectively and swinging it round while keeping one's footing on a wet scaffold, during heavy rain, was asking for mishaps.

Once the storm had ended, the executioner and his victim climbed the steps to the scaffold and prepared to play their different parts. The condemned woman knelt down and asked Sanson what she should do. He replied that she should arrange her hair so that it was piled up on her head, clear of her neck. She did so and then, just as he was whirling the sword around his head, Angelique Ticquet cried out, 'Be sure not to disfigure me!' This startled the executioner and his blow went awry, merely gashing the woman on the head. He was so taken aback by this, that it took him a further three blows to take off her head.

According to the Anglo-Saxon Chronicles, the earliest record of a judicial beheading was during the Roman occupation in AD 283. The incident involved a Christian priest who sought shelter with a young man called Alban. They both lived in the British city of Verulamium, not far from London. Christianity was being suppressed at this time, and the priest was in fear of his life. Alban not only let the man stay in his house, but he was converted and subsequently baptised by him. In order that the priest could escape, Alban suggested that they exchange clothes. The result was that Alban was sentenced to death and was beheaded with a sword on the site of what later became St Alban's Abbey.

For the next 800 years or so, beheading was used as an occasional punishment by the Anglo-Saxons and Vikings. It was not until William I invaded Britain in 1066 that decapitation became an established and respectable means of undergoing capital punishment. The first, named, victim was Waltheof, Earl of Northumberland, who had taken part in the Revolt of the Earls against William's rule. He was convicted of treason and paid the price for his rebellion at St Giles' Hill, near Winchester. He was beheaded with a sword on 31 May 1076. This began a very British tradition of cutting off the heads of noblemen and women who fell foul of the monarch; a tradition which was to last for the next 700 years.

Although beheading with a sword was not unknown in later years, by far the most common method of separating heads from bodies, at least in this country, was by means of an axe and block. The reasons for the use of this technique are purely practical. For one thing, using a sword to remove somebody's head requires the complete and willing cooperation of the victim. One must stand, or kneel, perfectly still, without moving a muscle. The sword itself must be heavy and razor sharp. Not only this, but the executioner must be very skilled and highly practised. There are many gruesome anecdotes, like the one at the beginning of this chapter, of victims who moved at the wrong moment or executioners who slipped on a wet scaffold. On the plus side, when such executions were carried out skilfully and without mishap, they could be very neat. There is a, perhaps apocryphal, story of one of the Sanson dynasty, who were the hereditary executioners of France. He was supposedly executing a nobleman who insisted on standing upright for the process, as he objected to dying on his knees. Sanson swept the sword round his head and it passed effortlessly through the man's neck. He remained standing, however, with his head still in place, balanced on the stump of his neck. It is said that Sanson murmured to him, 'Shake yourself monsieur, the job is done'.

The beauty of the British system is that it required brute strength, rather than skill and finesse. Neither did it matter if the condemned person fainted at the last moment; the neck was secure and in a convenient position. Another benefit was that an execution by axe and block could be undertaken effectively by any able-bodied man, without prior training; this was neatly demonstrated in March 1330. Roger Mortimer had assumed the position of dictator in Britain, although nominally acting on behalf of the teenage King Edward III. Feeling threatened by the King's uncle, Edmund, Duke of Kent, Mortimer had him arrested on a trumped up charge of treason. The duke was swiftly sentenced to death and his execution was supposed to follow immediately. He was led out in the presence of a body of soldiers, and prepared himself for death. However, a hitch occurred. Because he was the King's uncle, the executioner refused to behead him on the grounds that it might later be construed as an act of treason. Roger Mortimer then ordered an ordinary soldier to chop off the duke's head, but he too refused. Not one of the soldiers would agree to have anything to do with the execution; even the officers refused to act. Mortimer then sent to the prison to see if anybody at all would wield the axe; but there were no takers.

Several hours passed with messengers going back and forth, but still no executioner could be found. It was beginning to look as though Roger Mortimer might have to undertake the job himself. Eventually, however, by offering a pardon to anybody, under sentence of death themselves, who would cut off the Duke's head, a volunteer was found. He was a latrine cleaner who was due to be hanged the next day. In exchange for his release, he was handed the axe and told to get on with it. With no prior experience at all, he managed to remove the Duke of Kent's head with only one stroke.

Two different blocks were used for beheadings in this country; the low and the high. The high block was preferred by most victims. It consisted of a 2ft-high block of hardwood with concave depressions scooped out on either side. The advantage of the high block for the victim was that one was able to kneel gracefully and then simply lay one's head on the block, without having to sprawl across the scaffold in an undignified fashion. The low block was used in cases where resistance was expected, and when it might be necessary to hold the condemned person in place. It was seldom more than a foot high, making it necessary for victims to lie stretched out on their stomachs. This certainly looked less elegant than kneeling. It was also harder for the executioner to swing the axe at the correct angle.

We touch here upon a very remarkable aspect of British beheadings; it was assumed that those about to lose their heads would play their assigned part sportingly and not cut-up rough or struggle. It helped that most of those put to death like this belonged to a class with very fixed ideas about how to behave. It was also an advantage that many of the men had taken part in wars, and were expected to face death with a little more detachment than the average person. Even so, the ritual was heavily dependent on the assumption that everybody concerned – from headsman to victim – would behave properly and observe the rules of the game. On the rare occasions that these conventions were not observed, the consequences were disastrous. Take the case of Margaret Pole, Countess of Salisbury, for instance.

Margaret Pole came from a very ancient and aristocratic family. She was a lady-in-waiting of Henry VIII's first wife, Catherine of Aragon. Life during Henry's reign was like a bizarre game of snakes and ladders, and the Countess of Salisbury had the misfortune to slide down one of the longer snakes. Her son became a Roman Catholic cardinal, after Henry VIII's break with Rome, and this ultimately led to his mother's imprisonment and death.

After the failed Catholic uprising, which became known as the Pilgrimage of Grace, in which her son was implicated, the Countess of Salisbury was sent to the Tower of London. On 27 May 1541, she was told that she had been sentenced to death in her absence and was to die that morning. She was sixty-seven years old and, by all accounts, becoming a little vague. It is by no means impossible that she was suffering from Alzheimer's disease. At any rate, the scene on the scaffold was ghastly. The woman did not seem to realise what was happening to her. Instead of kneeling and allowing the headsman to do his job, she wandered around the scaffold distractedly, refusing point-blank to lay her head on the block. There is some dispute about the precise sequence of events. Some claim that the elderly Countess was pursued around the block by the executioner, who eventually hacked off her head. Others say that she had to be held in place, struggling frantically, on the block. What is not in dispute is that the first swing of the axe merely gashed her shoulder. It took a further ten strokes to remove her head!

The eleven blows needed to remove the Countess of Salisbury's head might be a British record, but it pales into insignificance beside some continental executions. In 1626, Count Henri de Chalais became involved in a plot to assassinate King Louis XIII of France. He was sentenced to be beheaded; the business to be carried out by the traditional French method, using a sword. It took an almost unbelievable twenty-nine strokes to remove the Count's head, and witnesses were certain that it was not until the twentieth blow that he stopped showing any signs of life.

The great majority of beheadings in this country took only one blow of the axe; this type of execution depending upon physical strength rather than any sort of skill. A heavy axe, swung over the head at a stationery target, will deliver more than enough force to cut through a human neck, provided of course that it is sharp enough. The perils of a blunt axe were neatly illustrated in 1685, during the execution of Charles II's illegitimate son, the Duke of Monmouth.

The Duke of Monmouth led a rebellion in the West Country, attempting to overthrow his uncle, James II. He was convicted of treason and his execution took place at the Tower of London, on 15 July 1685. When he walked up the steps to the scaffold, the first thing he did was pick up the axe and run his finger along the edge. At once, he expressed the fear that it was not sharp enough. The executioner, Jack Ketch, whose name has become synonymous with hangmen and executioners, reassured him. The Duke was still dubious, but nevertheless tipped the headsman with a purse containing seven guineas. It was customary to do this, in the same way that we might tip a barber or hairdresser today. As he handed over the purse, he told Ketch, 'Pray do not serve me as you did my Lord Russell. I have heard you struck him four or five times; if you strike me twice, I cannot promise you not to stir.' This was reference to a recent execution which had taken place in London. Once again, the executioner assured him that everything was fine.

The Duke of Monmouth's misgivings were soon shown to be justified. The first blow of the axe glanced off the back of his head, and he turned round to glare reproachfully at the man wielding the axe. After another two strokes, the Duke's head was still attached to his body and Jack Ketch threw down his axe, declaring that he could not continue with the job. What the Duke of Monmouth was feeling during all this can only be imagined. It is a great tribute to the British stiff upper-lip that he was able to wait patiently with his head on the block during this proceeding. The Sheriff told the headsman sternly that he had better continue what he had started. The wretched man then struck twice more, before finishing the job off with a knife!

After the Duke of Monmouth's head had been cut off, the Keeper of the King's Pictures suddenly realised that he had no official portrait of the executed man. Beheaded as a convicted traitor he may have been, but he had still been the son of King Charles II and nephew of the present king. It seemed wrong to leave such a gap in the pictorial history of the House of Stuart, and so the Duke's head was quickly stitched back onto his neck, and his corpse propped up in a chair. Sir Godfrey Kneller, the German-born portrait painter, was then summoned to record the Duke of Monmouth for posterity.

Few executions were as gruesome as the examples given above. In most cases, the man who was to suffer had practiced his lines and many came up with witty remarks for the occasion. Walter Raleigh, for instance, asked to see the axe and then, like the Duke of Monmouth, ran his finger over the edge. He smiled grimly, saying casually, 'It is a sharp medicine, but a sure remedy for all ills.' Thomas More went one better than this with not one but two grim jokes. He asked for a hand when mounting the scaffold, saying to an official, 'I pray you Mr Lieutenant, see me safe up and as for my coming down, let me shift for myself.' When the time came to lay his head on the block, he ostentatiously moved his beard out of the way, saying that as he knew of no treason that his beard had committed; it was a shame for it to suffer the same penalty as he faced himself.

There were a few recognised places for public executions in Britain. One of the most popular was the area around the Tower of London. For private executions, Tower Green, which was actually within the grounds of the Tower of London, was popular. For more public occasions, Tower Hill was used. Of course, the vicinity of the Tower was not the only place in London for beheadings. Lincoln's Inn Fields was also used for this purpose, as was Tyburn. South of the river, Kennington Common was a popular spot for beheadings, while Charles I was executed in Whitehall. Although most important beheadings took place in London, it was by no means uncommon for aristocratic prisoners to be executed in other cities, such as York. Because of the portability of the instruments needed to undertake this mode of execution, beheading could really be done anywhere. Perhaps the most important decapitation that this country has ever known, that of the reigning monarch, took place not at Tower Green, nor even within the Tower of London itself. Instead, it was staged in the very heart of Westminster; outside the banqueting house in Whitehall. Since this was such an important beheading and has several curious features, we shall examine it in detail.

At the end of the English Civil War in 1647, Charles I was held by the Parliamentary forces. While in captivity, he engaged in secret negotiations with the Scots, encouraging them to invade England. This triggered the Second Civil War, and brought home to those holding him that it was never going to be possible to release the King. The decision was accordingly made to put him on trial for treason. Kings of England had been deposed before, and done to death, but these had always been hole-and-corner affairs; murder, rather than judicial execution. The trial of Charles I was quite different. He was accused of treason against the English people, by putting his own personal interests above those of his subjects. This is not the place to go into the legality of such a move, which has been hotly debated over the succeeding centuries, but on Saturday, 27 January 1649, Charles Stuart was found guilty and sentenced to death by beheading.

He was returned to St James' Palace for a few days, until arrangements had been made for his execution. There is still uncertainty as to the identity of the man who actually took off the king's head. It is said that Richard Brandon, the London hangman, was offered the job, but refused. There are claims though, that Brandon admitted on his deathbed that he had, indeed, carried out the execution. Other accounts suggest that two relatively inexperienced men were engaged for the job at £100 each. Whatever the truth, the executioner and his assistant both wore masks on the scaffold. In view of the vengeance wrought upon all connected with the trial, following the restoration of the monarchy in 1660, this was probably a shrewd move.

On the morning of Tuesday, 30 January, the king was escorted by soldiers from St James' Palace to Whitehall. A scaffold had been erected at first-floor height, so that it was necessary to enter the Banqueting House, climb the stairs, and then step out of one of the windows onto the scaffold itself. A low block was used for the execution of Charles I, and he realised at once that this would force him to lay full length on the straw-covered floor. He was to remark on this later, but first made sure that the executioner would allow him to give the signal for his own death. He told the sinister, masked figure, 'I shall say but very short prayers and when I thrust out my hands...'

He then indicated his long, flowing hair and asked, 'Does my hair trouble you?' For a clean beheading, at one stroke, it was necessary to have an unobstructed part of the bare neck at which to strike. Following the advice given, he then tucked his hair into a cap. He exchanged a few words with Bishop Juxton, who had accompanied him onto the scaffold, saying, 'I go from a corruptible to an incorruptible crown.'

It was almost time for the closing scene of the tragedy that had been the English Civil War. After asking the executioner, 'Is my hair well?' the king looked dubiously at the low block, saying, 'You must set it fast', to which the man replied, 'It is fast, Sire.' Charles then said somewhat peevishly, 'It might have been a little higher.' The executioner was embarrassed and told him apologetically, 'It can be no higher, Sire'. Nobody wished to explain to the king that the reason for the low block was born out of concern over the extent to which he would cooperate with his own execution. Provisional plans had been made for binding him and securing him to the scaffold, with iron staples! In the words of a contemporary writer:

> It must be dreadfully remembered, that the cruel powers did suspect that the king would not submit his head to the block, and therefore to bring him

down to violence to it, they had prepared hooks and staples to haul him as a victim to the slaughter.

Still not entirely satisfied, the king told the headsman, 'When I put out my hands this way then...' at the same time demonstrating how he would give the sign.

Charles then laid his head on the block and began to pray. Hearing the executioner shifting his weight from one foot to the other, and thinking that the man was about to strike, he warned him, 'Stay for the sign'. The headsman assured him, 'I will and it please your Majesty.' A few seconds later, the king stretched out his arms and the axe came down, severing his head cleanly with one blow. His head dropped into the zinc-lined basket placed to receive it. Except for the use of the low, rather than high block, this execution was typical of this type of death.

The procedure for executions by beheading followed the same general pattern, no matter where and when they took place. To begin with, they were, as mentioned above, reserved in the main for nobility. Commoners might be granted this type of death, but only as a favour. Mark Smeaton, a musician at the court of Henry VIII, was such a person. He was convicted of having an adulterous affair with Ann Boleyn, which normally would have brought a sentence of hanging, drawing and quartering for treason. This was the accepted penalty for commoners. However, since Smeaton cooperated fully during his interrogation, he was granted the favour of being beheaded instead. He was put to death at Tyburn, where common criminals were disposed of, instead of Tower Hill.

On conviction, the prisoner might not be executed at once. King Charles spent only three days under sentence of death before his execution, but this was fairly unusual. Those trying him knew that he represented a deadly threat and wished to be rid of him, as soon as was practicable. Sir Walter Raleigh was, after being sentenced to death, held prisoner in the Tower of London for thirteen years; his execution only taking place fifteen years after the original sentence of death had been pronounced. This was admittedly an extreme case, but it was not uncommon for a condemned prisoner to spend a year or two in the Tower, while the monarch decided whether or not to spare his life. We saw earlier the dreadful execution of the Countess of Salisbury. In her case, sentence of death had been passed in 1539, but it was not until 1541 that the execution actually took place. This was a common delay.

This was in sharp contrast to the execution of common criminals; those sentenced to hang for murder or theft. In such cases, the hanging typically took place within a few days, or at the most weeks, of the conviction. Those awaiting death by beheading might easily spend years in captivity, never knowing when the date with the headsman would come. It must have been a tremendous psychological strain. One would go to bed each night for perhaps years on end, without knowing whether or not that day was one's last.

Margaret Pole, the Countess of Salisbury, was not told until the morning of her death that she was to be executed that day. Again, this was fairly typical.

Noble prisoners, under sentence of death, were treated with all the respect due to their status in society. Guards would address them by their correct title, even, in the case of Charles I on the scaffold, as 'Sire' or 'Your Majesty'. The whole proceeding was very polite and formal. There was almost invariably an opportunity for the condemned person to make a short speech to the witnesses, before the execution took place. In a surprising number of cases, the victim praised the mercy of the monarch and acknowledged the justice of the sentence. There were sound practical reasons for this. Most of those who were to be executed in this way were leaving behind high profile families. If it was suspected by the establishment that the noble family left behind felt aggrieved by the court's verdict, or angry that their relative had not received a pardon from the King, then those people might themselves be seen as a threat to the Crown. By abasing themselves, and agreeing that it was right and proper that they should die for their crimes, the condemned person hoped to avert any future action being taken against those whom they left behind. The repentance displayed by these people, and their evident devotion to the monarch are quite astonishing. John Dudley, Duke of Northumberland, said before he was beheaded for treason in 1553, 'I have deserved one thousand deaths.' Thomas Cromwell, staunch friend of Henry VIII before falling from favour, declared:

> The devil is ready to seduce us and I have been seduced, but bear witness that I die in the Catholic faith of the Holy Church and I heartily desire you to pray for the King's grace, that he may long live with you in health and prosperity and after him that his son Edward, may long reign over you.

The Earl of Essex, a favourite of Elizabeth I who led an abortive rebellion against her, said before he laid his head on the block:

> In humility and obedience to thy commandments, in obedience to thy ordinance and good pleasure, Oh God I prostrate myself to my deserved punishment.

These were just the kind of sentiments which might persuade a revengeful king or queen to spare the family of an executed man.

An exception to these pious and self-serving speeches was the final address of the Scottish noblemen, who rebelled against the Hanoverian Kings in the early eighteenth century. So fierce was their devotion to the Stuart cause, and so great the detestation which they felt for the, as they saw it, Germans who had seized the throne, that they could not bring themselves to mouth the usual platitudes expected under such circumstances. They believed that James II's son was in fact James III of Britain and that his son, Charles, was the heir to the throne. On the scaffold, shortly before he was beheaded in 1746, Lord Balmerino made a speech in which he referred openly to 'King James'. He probably guessed, rightly, there was little point in paying lip service to the House of Hanover at that late stage!

The Scottish lords were admired for their good-natured banter, which they maintained to the end. This was seen as being the correct thing to do; to go to one's death with a jest, combined with a proper degree of resignation. Simon Fraser, the 11th Lord Lovat, joked with the headsman, telling him that he would be angry if the man failed to remove his head at one stroke. Although a remarkably unpleasant individual, even his enemies were forced to admire his courage and good nature during the execution. One biographer said that though he had lived like a fox, he at least died like a lion. He was eighty years old and very fat; needing the assistance of two men to mount the steps to the scaffold. He noticed the huge number of spectators and laughed, saying:

God save us, why should there be such a bustle about taking off an old grey head that cannot get up three steps without three bodies to support it?

There were of course degrees of nobility. This was reflected in the location chosen for the beheading. In London, as we have seen, the vicinity of the Tower of London was popular for executions by beheading. These could take place either publicly or privately. Tower Hill was the place for public decapitation and anybody could come and watch. The crowds at such events could be immense. At Lord Lovat's execution (he was, incidentally, the last person to die by beheading in this country), stands were erected to accommodate those wishing to watch the entertainment. Contemporary illustrations show them to be like the grandstands at a football ground. One of these stands collapsed while Lord Lovat was giving his speech, causing him to remark in an aside, 'The more mischief the merrier'. Twelve people were killed.

Private beheadings took place within the grounds of the Tower of London, on Tower Green. 'Private' is something of a misnomer really, for many dozens of people were often present. Indeed, at some executions within the Tower, upwards of 150 spectators were present. Women were almost invariably executed within the grounds of the Tower of London. The reason was simple. The sight of a woman having her head hacked off, with all the goriness which this entailed, was thought likely to provoke sympathy for the victim, no matter what she had done. This might be translated into criticism of the monarch, who allowed such a thing to happen. The two wives of Henry VIII who were beheaded, Ann Boleyn and Katherine Howard, were both executed privately on Tower Green. So was the seventeen-year-old Lady Jane Grey, who was manipulated by her family into becoming a pretender to the throne. She was beheaded in the precincts of the Tower of London in 1554.

In the case of Ann Boleyn, the king was worried that even a private execution might not be enough to prevent sympathy for the disgraced queen. There was a discussion with his advisors as to the ramifications of forcing a former queen to kneel down and lay her head on the block. A compromise was reached, whereby instead of using an axe, Ann's head would be removed with a sword. As has already been mentioned, decapitating somebody with a sword is a lot trickier than using an axe. A great deal of skill and a lot of practice is required to wield a beheading sword effectively. There had been no such execution in Britain in living memory and so it was thought wise to send to the continent, where this technique had been flourishing for many years.

The beheading sword, used widely in Europe, was about 3ft long and weighed around 4lbs. Its blade was wide and ended in a blunt tip; there was no need for a sharp point. This was a double-handed weapon and the grip was covered in rough leather or fish skin. The executioner would whirl the sword around his head once or twice, before slicing through the victim's neck. The condemned prisoners either knelt upright or were seated in chairs. It was essential that they did not move throughout the whole performance. There are ghastly tales of victims having the top of their heads removed like boiled eggs, because they flinched at the wrong moment.

At the time of Ann Boleyn's execution, the French city of Calais was still an English possession. An emissary of the court was accordingly dispatched to seek out a top-class executioner for the projected job. They interviewed Jean Rombaud for the post, and he offered to prove his skill in the next few days. Two men lay under sentence of death, and Rombaud decided that while executing them he would provide a virtuoso display of technical skill for the Englishmen offering such an important commission. He arranged for the two condemned men to be seated blindfold in chairs, facing away from each other. He stood between the chairs, whirled the mighty sword around his head a couple of times before cutting off the heads of both men with one sweep. He was awarded the contract on the spot.

Ann Boleyn was beheaded on 19 May 1536. The raised wooden scaffold was set up in the precincts of the Tower of London, which afforded a degree of privacy. There were, however, many witnesses. The executioner was disconcerted by the beauty of the doomed former queen, and felt so sorry for her that he devised a cunning scheme to make her passing as easy as possible. He kept his double-handed sword hidden from view under some of the straw which covered the scaffold. When all was ready and his victim was kneeling upright, blindfolded and with her hair piled up, clear of her neck; Rombaud quietly picked up the sword and prepared to strike. He then scuffed his feet and asked in a stage whisper to be handed his sword. As he did so Ann Boleyn, who was praying quietly, turned her head slightly, thinking that she still had a second or two to live. At that moment, the Frenchman brought his sword sweeping down in a glittering arc, severing the head from the body in one blow.

The executioner lifted the head up high in the air to show it to the crowd. Some witnesses swore that Ann Boleyn's lips were still moving in prayer. This sounds at first like some fanciful legend which might have arisen over the centuries. Curiously though, there are many such stories associated with decapitations. Indeed, precisely the same thing is said to have happened at the execution of Waltheof, which we touched upon earlier in this chapter. He too was praying when decapitated by a sword and it is related that he too continued with his prayer for a few seconds after his head was struck off. There are so many similar accounts of this phenomenon, including many from the mass use of the guillotine during the French Revolution, that a number of scientists have speculated upon the possibility of consciousness remaining after a head has been cut off. The most detailed investigation of this idea was carried out in France, in the early twentieth century.

In 1906, a fascinating experiment was conducted by Dr Ronald Marcoux, a surgeon who had obtained permission to study the corpses of guillotined men. His findings are reported in the *Archives d'Anthroplogie Criminelle*, Paris, 1906. On 28 August 1906, a cold-blooded killer called Magret was guillotined. Dr Marcoux, who was present at the execution, approached the basket containing the severed head only a second or two after the blade had fallen. Magret's head lay face up, with the eyes closed. Dr Marcoux leaned into the basket, until he was only a few inches from the gruesome object, and said in a loud voice, 'Magret'. Immediately, the eyes opened and gazed into those of the astonished doctor. For ten seconds or so, the two men looked into each others eyes. Then Magret's eyes closed. Then the eyes of the unattached head opened, once again, and looked keenly at Dr Marcoux before they then turned and stared intently at the blood-spattered blade of the guillotine.

Dr Marcoux was absolutely convinced that Magret's head had been conscious and aware for at least fifteen or twenty seconds after it had been cut from the body. The preliminary report of his findings was not at all popular with the authorities, and he was refused permission to conduct any further experiments of the sort.

It is quite probable that consciousness would be retained for a few seconds after decapitation. To remain alert, the brain needs a constant supply of fresh, oxygenated blood. There would be enough oxygen in the blood circulating in the head to maintain functioning of the brain for a short while. After all, when the supply of blood to the brain is cut off by pressure being applied to the carotid artery, when somebody is being choked for example, even with no fresh blood being able to flow into the brain, loss of consciousness is not instantaneous.

There is a natural reluctance to dwell unduly on the physical details of beheading. Eyewitness accounts of the process are revolting. Take the matter of blood pressure. The blood in the body is kept at a fairly high pressure. This is necessary so that efficient circulation may be maintained under any circumstances in which the body should find itself – upside down, laying flat and so on. A natural consequence of this is that when the head is removed, the blood under pressure is shot out some distance, just like any other pressurised system springing a leak. While the heart continues to pump, blood can be sprayed 6ft from the body. This is why the scaffold was liberally spread with straw.

Very few women were beheaded, even when it was common to end the lives of traitors in this way. For those who were executed by this method, it was almost always a private affair, taking place behind the closed walls of the Tower of London or another prison. The last beheading of a woman in this country was, however, an exception to this rule.

Dame Alice Lisle, a seventy-one-year-old widow, lived in Dorset. Her husband, John, had been the man entrusted by Oliver Cromwell to arrange the trial of the deposed king of England – Charles I. When the monarchy was restored in 1660, John Lisle thought it prudent to slip into exile in Switzerland, where he was later murdered. His wife retired to the West Country to live out her days in peace and quiet, far from the bustle of London. This was her plan at least, but Charles II's illegitimate son James, Duke of Monmouth, had plans of his own. In the summer of 1685, he attempted to lead an army of peasants from Somerset and Dorset to march on London and overthrow his uncle, King James II. His scheme came to nothing and after his defeat at the Battle of Sedgemoor, his followers fled wherever they could.

One of the fugitives fleeing the scene after the Duke of Monmouth's abortive bid for power was his chaplain, John Hicks. Together with a man called Richard Nelthorp, he sought refuge at Alice Lisle's house on 28 July, where she sheltered and fed them. The next day, Colonel Penruddock, the local JP, arrived with a party of soldiers and arrested the two men, along with Dame Alice. It was a very bad time to be accused of giving comfort to Monmouth and his rebels. King James had despatched the notorious Judge Jeffreys to the area, to wreak vengeance on those who had tried to overthrow him. Jeffreys held a series of trials which became known as the 'Bloody Assizes', notable for the number of death sentences and transportations of men to the American colonies. These trials began at Winchester on 25 August 1685.

It was obvious from the beginning that Judge Jeffreys was not planning on acquitting any of those brought before his court for offences connected with the unsuccessful rising. One of the first to face him in the dock was Alice Lisle, a deaf old woman who had done no more than allow a couple of exhausted men to spend the night at her house. The charge against her was:

> That on July 28th, knowing that one John Hicks, clerk to the false traitor and to have conspired to the death and destruction of the King, and to have levied war against him, did, in her dwelling house at Ellingham, Dorset, trai-

torously entertain, conceal and comfort the said John Hicks and cause meat
and drink to be delivered to him, against her allegiance to the King.

A very interesting legal point was now raised. Since John Hicks had yet to be
tried and convicted of treason, was it possible to convict Alice Lisle of harbouring a traitor? Surely at the very least, Hicks would first have to be proved
a traitor himself. Judge Jeffreys swept aside this objection and the trial began.

The evidence against Dame Alice was slight enough. Although she admitted that she knew that a warrant had been issued for the arrest of Hicks, she
claimed not to know that he was a member of Monmouth's forces. She also
pointed out that her own son was serving in the army. The jury returned for
the first time, saying that they did not believe that Dame Alice was aware that
Hicks was associated with the Duke of Monmouth. Judge Jeffreys sent them
back to deliberate again. A short time later, they returned to deliver a formal
verdict of 'Not Guilty'. Again, the judge sent them off to consider his strong
judicial recommendation that the woman was plainly guilty of treason. It was
neither the time nor the place to appear to be favouring a traitor, and so the
jury came back with the 'correct' verdict of 'Guilty'.

Lord Macaulay, the famous essayist, wrote the pithiest account of this trial
ever to appear. He said:

> If Lady Alice knew her guests to have been concerned in the insurrection,
> she was undoubtedly guilty of what in strictness is a capital crime. The feel-
> ing which makes the most loyal subject shrink from the thought of giving
> up to a shameful death the rebel who, vanquished, hunted down, and in
> mortal agony, begs for a morsel of bread and a cup of water though, may
> be a weakness: but it is surely a weakness very nearly allied to virtue. No
> English ruler who has been thus baffled, the savage and implacable James
> II alone excepted, has had the barbarity even to think of putting a lady to a
> cruel and shameful death for so venial and amiable a transgression.
>
> Odious as the law was, it was strained for the purpose of destroying Alice
> Lisle. Witnesses prevaricated; the jury, consisting of the principal gentlemen
> of Hampshire, shrank from the thought of sending a fellow creature to the
> stake for conduct which seemed deserving rather of praise than of blame.
> Jeffreys was beside himself with fury. He stormed, cursed, and swore in lan-
> guage which no well-bred man would have used at a race or a cockfight.
>
> The jury retired, and remained long in consultation. The judge grew
> impatient. He could not conceive, he said, how, in so plain a case, they
> should even have left the box. He sent a messenger to tell them that, if they
> did not instantly return, he would adjourn the court and lock them up all
> night. Thus put to the torture, they came, but came to say that they doubted
> whether the charge had been made out. Jeffreys expostulated with them

vehemently, and, after another consultation, they gave a reluctant verdict of Guilty.

The official punishment for women convicted of treason was burning at the stake. Judge Jeffreys warned the wretched woman that she was to burn that very afternoon and urged her to confess. There was actually a week's respite, during which time James II commuted the sentence to beheading.

On 2 September, the execution of this old woman took place in the most public place imaginable; the marketplace in Winchester. The aim was to strike fear into the hearts of anybody whose loyalty to King James might be wavering. It is hard to avoid the suspicion that, in addition to the charge of which she had been convicted, here too was an opportunity for the monarchy to revenge itself upon the widow of the man who had, in part, been responsible for the execution of King James' father, some forty years earlier. Dame Alice Lisle conducted herself with great dignity, laying her head calmly upon the block. Her head was removed cleanly with one stroke of the axe. She was the last woman in this country to be executed in this way.

By the time that Alice Lisle was beheaded in Winchester marketplace, this type of execution was already becoming something of an anachronism. It was, nevertheless, to be over sixty years before the last judicial beheading took place. There were occasional executions by this method in the late seventeenth and early eighteenth centuries, but it was not until the mid-eighteenth century, in the aftermath of the Scottish uprising of 1745, that there was a final flurry of beheadings which signalled the end of the practice.

On 18 August 1746, the Earl of Kilmarnock and Lord Balmerino were both beheaded on the same day. The Earl of Kilmarnock was repentant and sad, but Balmerino was as boisterous as though he were visiting a tavern. He had been dining with his wife when the warrant for his execution had arrived at the Tower, where he was a prisoner. The Lord Lieutenant insisted on reading it aloud, whereupon Lord Balmerino's wife sprang to her feet and swooned. Balmerino angrily reproached the man reading the warrant, saying, 'With your damned warrant, you have spoiled my lady's dinner.'

When he climbed up to the scaffold, which had been erected on Tower Hill, he noticed his coffin lying to one side. He showed great interest in this, taking the time to read the inscription out loud. The headsman was unnerved by Balmerino's sangfroid, and when he approached the Scottish lord to beg forgiveness in the customary manner, he looked genuinely dejected and unhappy about the whole business. Lord Balmerino tried to cheer him up by slapping him on the back, and tipping him with the then enormous sum of three guineas. It took three blows to sever his head from his body.

And so to Lord Lovatt, the last man to have his head removed in this way. Lord Lovatt had already gained a reputation for his repartee. On the way to his trial for treason, his carriage was held up and a woman in the crowd shouted to him, 'You ugly old dog, don't you think you will have that frightful head cut off?' Quick as flash, he shot back, 'You damned ugly old bitch, I do believe I shall!'

On the morning of his execution, 9 April 1747, Lord Lovatt rose at about 5 a.m. and spent a good deal of time in prayer. He ate a very good breakfast of minced veal and invited some friends to have coffee, while he himself had a glass of wine. He was at that time eighty, and so fat that it was necessary for him to stop and rest after walking even a short distance. The entire proceedings were conducted with great civility on all sides, with the Lord thanking those around him for their help and they in turn apologising for what was about to happen. Some of his friends were allowed to accompany him right up onto the scaffold. When he noticed that one of the men looked unhappy, he laughed and made an effort to cheer him up. He gave the executioner a purse containing ten guineas, and then indicated that he would pray for a short time with his head on the block, before giving the headsman the signal by dropping a handkerchief. He did so, and despite his fatness, the executioner managed to take off his head with one stroke of the axe. Indeed, the blade of the axe not only passed through Lord Lovatt's neck, it embedded itself 2in into the block as well. The axe and block used for this execution is now on display in the Tower of London.

The ultimate destination of the heads removed from the traitors is an interesting study in itself. Not everybody could be present at the execution, and so it was arranged that at least their heads could be seen, as evidence that they had paid the price for their treason. At the time, London Bridge had many shops and houses along its length, rather like the present-day Ponte Vecchio in Florence. At the Southwark end of the bridge, guarding the crossing to the walled city of London, was a gatehouse. It was here that the Keeper of the Heads had his official residence. His job was to make sure that the heads of executed men were properly displayed above the bridge's gatehouse. The ostensible idea was that these grim relics would act as a deterrent to those minded to conspire against the monarch; the heads above the gateway on London Bridge making a powerful statement to everybody who crossed the bridge. They would remain there for years at a time – the largest number ever counted at one time was thirty-four. In later years it became customary to boil the heads in a mixture of various spices, in order to discourage carrion birds from pecking them to pieces. They were sometimes coated with pitch for the same reason. Before this, however, there was a clear expectation that the flesh of the heads would, in fact, be eaten by the birds. The words of the death sentence imposed upon those guilty of treason made this quite clear. For those who were to be hanged, drawn and quartered, for instance, the death sentence ended with these words:

And lastly his body to be quartered and the quarters set up in some high and eminent place, to the view and detestation of men, and to become a prey for the fowls of the air.

Separating the head from the body and ensuring that they would never be reunited, was also an integral part of the punishment. In an age which confidently expected a physical resurrection of the body on the day of Judgement, the idea that a person might be buried without his head was a shocking one, with implications for eternity!

Viewing the heads on London Bridge was a Sunday afternoon entertainment for many poor people. It was roughly comparable to visiting Madame Tussauds' waxworks today; a chance to see the faces of people one would never get to meet in real life. The newly-installed head of a prominent person would always bring crowds out to admire it.

The bridge at Southwark was not the only place in London where severed heads were to be seen. One of the points at which the City of Westminster ends, and London begins, was in Fleet Street. A gateway stood here from the fourteenth century onwards, and it was felt that displaying the heads, and other parts of executed traitors, here, might perhaps also be a good idea. The old gateway was demolished in the seventeenth century and Sir Christopher Wren, architect of St Paul's Cathedral, was commissioned to design a new one.

The gateway at Temple Bar, which was completed in 1672, was a perfect, miniature gem of English baroque architecture. It was also, sited as it was at a main thoroughfare into the City of London, the perfect spot to put on show the heads of executed traitors. A few years after it was completed, the gateway at Temple Bar was first used for the display of decapitated heads and other, even more gruesome body parts.

In 1683, a plan to assassinate Charles II and his brother, the Duke of York, was foiled. The Rye House Plot, as it became known, resulted in the execution of several high-profile victims, including Lord Russell, who was beheaded in Lincolns Inn fields. Other conspirators were hanged, drawn and quartered. The heads, and also quarters of bodies, were stuck on long iron spikes and used to decorate the top of the Temple Bar. The heads of those found guilty of plotting against William III were also stuck on pikes and displayed here. In 1716, and again in 1722, the heads of traitors were fixed atop the Temple Bar gateway. The head fixed there in 1722 actually belonged to a man who had been hanged, rather than beheaded. Christopher Layer was a young barrister who lived in Chancery Lane. He became involved in the Atterbury Plot; an attempt to drive George I from the throne by inviting French troops to occupy London. It was as plain a case of treason as one could wish to see and Layer was hanged at Tyburn. After his death, his head was removed and brought to the Temple Bar for display.

The last heads to be placed on show in this way were those of men who had taken part in the 1745 rebellion. We have read of the Scottish lords who were beheaded on Tower Hill. Many others were also executed for their part in this final effort to overthrow the House of Hanover. Among them were nine men who had taken arms against the Crown – a capital offence. Colonel Francis Townley was one of these and, together with eight other rebels, he was sentenced to be hanged, drawn and quartered. This was carried out on Kennington Common. The full rigours of this horrible sentence were not enacted upon the condemned men; they were allowed to hang for over half an hour, until they were all dead. A fire was then kindled and they were disembowelled, beheaded and quartered. Their bowels were thrown into the fire. A truly ghastly incident occurred during this revolting procedure. A soldier called Buckhorse took a piece of Townley's flesh and ate it raw, as a demonstration of his loyalty to the king. Nor was this the only unexpected event of the day. The fiancée of one of the men put to death that day came to witness his execution. James Dawson's intended bride cried out, as his bowels were thrown into the fire, 'My dear, I follow thee – I follow thee! Lord God, receive our souls, I pray Thee!' To everybody's horror, she then fell dead on the spot.

Colonel Townley's head, and that of a man called Fletcher, were then treated with tar to preserve them and skewered on long iron rods, so that they could be clearly seen on top of Wren's gateway. Horace Walpole, the well-known writer, recalled seeing a shopkeeper in Fleet Street, who was charging passersby a halfpenny a time to look at the heads through a miniature telescope.

The heads of Townley and Fletcher went up above Temple Bar on 12 August 1746. Incredibly, they remained there for a quarter of a century, so securely attached were they to the iron rods holding them aloft. They finally fell down during a thunderstorm in 1772. One rolled along the street until it bumped into the ankles of a passing woman. She screamed and then fainted. The gateway at Temple Bar is still standing, although it has since been moved a couple of times, and may currently be seen next to St Paul's Cathedral.

Times were changing and there was something quite anachronistic about different styles of execution for different classes. As the Industrial Revolution gathered pace, it was clear that this whole business was an anomaly. In 1760, Earl Ferrers, a nobleman in whose family ran a streak of insanity, shot dead his steward. He demanded and received a trial by his fellow peers, which was held in Westminster Hall. Earl Ferrers pleaded insanity, but this was such a shocking and unpopular crime that the Lords found him guilty of murder. To his dismay, the Earl was sentenced to hang for this crime, just like anybody else. He petitioned to have the mode of execution changed to beheading, but to no avail. Peers were now subject to the same laws and similar penalties as everybody else. The only concession made to his noble birth was that permission was granted for him to be hanged with a silken rope, instead of the usual hemp!

I said earlier that Lord Lovatt's was the last case of beheading in this country, but this is not strictly true. In Chapter 7, we will be looking at the peculiarly British mode of execution known as hanging, drawing and quartering. This sentence lingered on, incredibly, until several years after the end of the Napoleonic Wars in the early nineteenth century. The Industrial Revolution was in full swing when last this ancient sentence was pronounced, on 28 April 1820. The sensitivities of Britain by that time, less than twenty years before Victoria ascended the throne, would not allow the full horrors of this form of execution to be enacted. It was commuted to hanging, followed by post-mortem decapitation.

The Cato Street Conspirators were a bunch of hare-brained idealists who hatched a mad plot to overthrow the government. There were only a handful of them, but nevertheless, they hoped to murder the cabinet and trigger a popular uprising. There was a good deal of political unrest at that time, and so, when they were arrested, it was decided to make an example of them – hence the trial for High Treason and sentence of hanging, drawing and quartering.

On the morning of 1 May 1820, five of the conspirators were hanged in front of Newgate Prison, on the site of the Old Bailey in London. After their bodies had been left hanging for an hour (to ensure that they were dead), the corpses were cut down and laid on the scaffold. The actual decapitations were carried out not by the executioner, John Foxton, but by a sinister figure wearing a mask. The rumour was that this was an impecunious medical student, who had volunteered to undertake this gory task for a few pounds. Another story suggested that the man removing the heads was actually a body-snatcher, who had been engaged because he had some experience of helping anatomists at their work. There was some disappointment in the crowd when it became clear that the heads of the five traitors were not to be removed with an axe, but by means of various scalpels and knives. It was a horrible business; not withstanding the fact that the men were dead, there was a great deal of blood. This led to an incident which cheered up the crowd, and made up for not seeing the swinging of an axe.

As the masked man removed the heads, he handed them to Foxton, who then held each up for the crowd to see, proclaiming in the time honoured formula, 'Behold the head of a traitor!' The third head was so slippery with blood that Foxton lost hold, and the gruesome object went rolling across the scaffold. There was a roar of laughter and cries of 'Butterfingers!' The mood of the crowd changed at once, from sullen disapproval at being cheated of a traditional beheading, into a kind of music-hall gaiety.

There was to be no further deliberate, judicial removal of heads in Britain after the execution of the Cato Street Conspirators. It was realised by those in power that the public mutilation of corpses had no place in a modern, industrial society.

Sixty-five years later, there was a brief and unsavoury coda to the history of beheading in Britain; a case of what one might perhaps call inadvertent decapitation. In Chapter 10, we shall be examining cases where a judicial punishment had resulted in *de facto* execution. We shall look now at a situation where one method of execution was prescribed by law, yet quite another ended up being inflicted on the victim.

On 15 September 1885, a market gardener called Robert Goodale argued fiercely with his wife Bathsheba. He lost patience with her, and ended up banging her around the head with a hatchet before throwing her into a well, where she drowned. It was not, therefore, wholly surprising when Robert Goodale found himself standing trial for murder at the Norfolk Assizes, which were held in Norwich on 13 November 1885. His trial, for what the press called 'The Walsoken Tragedy', took place before Mr Justice Stephen. The result was never seriously in doubt, and Goodale was sentenced to hang. He was removed to Norwich Castle, where his execution was scheduled to take place in the morning of 30 November.

A few words about Goodale might not come amiss at this point. First, he was a heavy man, weighing over 15 stones. He was very flabby and out of condition. He was also a great coward, who was terrified out of his wits at the prospect of being hanged. In the twentieth century, when the only witnesses to hangings in this country were officials who had signed the Official Secrets Act, it was possible to maintain the fiction that all executions were smoothly-conducted affairs, with the condemned men and women walking cheerfully to their deaths; the entire activity being conducted with as little fuss and discomfort as a visit to the dentist. The reality is that some of the scenes which took place at hangings, were worse than anybody's most hideous nightmare. Robert Goodale's execution was a gruesome spectacle; because reporters were allowed to be present at that time, we have several vivid, eyewitness descriptions of the full horror of the occasion.

The so-called 'Long Drop', intended to break the victim's neck rather than choke him to death, had been introduced to British hanging a few years before Goodale's execution. A table of drops had been compiled; the heavier the person, the shorter the drop needed. It was a fine balancing act, the aim being to use a sufficiently long drop to break the neck, while on the other hand not so long that the head was pulled off entirely.

According to the official chart, a man of Goodale's weight should have been given a drop of 7ft 8in. The hangman, James Berry, was worried though, because his observation of the condemned man suggested that his neck muscles were very weak. Berry accordingly reduced the length of the drop dramatically to 5ft 9in.

The problems which were to beset the execution of Robert Goodale began as soon as James Berry appeared in the condemned cell at a few minutes before eight o'clock on 30 November. It is sometimes forgotten that all executions rely, to a greater or lesser extent, upon the cooperation of the condemned person. At the very least, he is expected to get dressed on the day of his execution and walk to the place where his death will occur. When somebody is resolutely determined not to die, things can get very tricky. Berry later sold his memoirs to a newspaper, and there was also a reporter from the *Norfolk Chronicle* present during the execution. We have, as a result, a full and detailed account of the events that morning.

As the executioner approached the condemned cell, he could hear Goodale moaning and screaming in terror. The usual procedure was that Berry would enter the cell, shake hands with the condemned man and then pass a leather strap around his arms, pinioning them to his body. Goodale was a stout man, and struggled so violently that this proved to be impossible. The hangman simply could not hold Goodale's arms in place for long enough to fasten the buckle. The scene in the cell began to resemble a free for all, with warders sitting on the condemned man, trying to force his arms to his side so that Berry could do up the strap. After a minute or two, it became clear that this was not going to be possible, and the hangman asked one of the warders to go and find some wire. Eventually, by wrapping wire round the man, it was found possible to restrain his arms sufficiently for the next stage in the proceedings to be attempted – getting the condemned man to the gallows.

Between them, Berry and the warders, who had by now sent for help, managed to get the struggling man out of the cell and into the courtyard, where he caught sight of the gallows. At this point, Goodale redoubled his efforts and simply refused to move a single pace towards the waiting noose. The crowd outside the prison, who were waiting to see the raising of the black flag (which signified the death of the condemned man), were growing puzzled. Rumours spread that Goodale had somehow managed to cheat the hangman by committing suicide in the night. The truth was infinitely more horrible.

Once more, James Berry had to take charge of the situation. He ordered a warder to fetch a length of strong rope. At this point, one of the official witnesses turned pale and rushed off, unable to bear the scene any longer. When the rope was brought, Berry tied it round the fighting man and gave the ends to two warders; they then jerked and dragged Goodale towards the gallows. Some pushed and other pulled; somehow, it was found possible to get the man onto the scaffold. Warders held Goodale upright, while Berry fixed the noose round his neck. The warders then left the platform, upon which Goodale promptly collapsed in a heap. Berry persuaded one of the warders to help the fainting man stand upright, and then swiftly pulled the lever to operate the trapdoor. To his horror, he saw that the warder had not been able to jump clear in time and very nearly plunged into the pit with Goodale. At the last moment, the man was able to grasp onto the edge of the drop.

The other witnesses though had noticed something even more disturbing than the warder's slowness in getting clear of the drop. As Goodale fell through the trapdoors, the rope snapped tight and then jerked loosely upwards; evidently with nothing on the end of it. What had happened to Goodale? Had the rope snapped under his weight? Or had the noose slipped over his head? It was neither of these. When the hangman went to investigate, he found to his horrified amazement that the rope had actually cut through Goodale's neck, as cleanly as a knife. Lying on the floor of the pit was Goodale's headless body, with his decapitated head lying a few feet away. The place was awash with blood.

It was apparent that Robert Goodale's neck muscles were considerably weaker than James Berry had thought them to be. Although the inquest on the dead man cleared Berry of all blame, the 'Goodale Mess', as it became known, had a profound effect upon him. It also led, in the course of time, to a more scientific way of calculating the required drop necessary to break a person's neck cleanly, without severing the head completely. Robert Goodale deserves a minor footnote in the annals of British capital punishment, as the last person in this country to be executed by the removal of his head.

A final historical curiosity is that judicial beheading remained a possibility in this country right up until the late twentieth century. The penalty of hanging, drawing and quartering was abolished by the 1870 Forfeiture Act, which made ordinary hanging the mandatory sentence for High Treason. Whether by oversight or otherwise, the 1870 Act did not remove the right of the monarch to substitute decapitation for hanging. The death penalty for treason was not removed from the statute book until the passing of the 1998 Crime and Disorder Act, and so until that year it was technically possible for traitors to be hanged. However, until 1973, they could instead, at least in theory, be decapitated if this was the express wish of the reigning monarch. In that year, section 2 of the 1814 Treason Act was repealed by the Statute Law (Repeals) Act 1973. It was only from that time onwards, three quarters of the way through the twentieth century, that beheading was finally removed from the statute book.

THE RISE OF HANGING

We have seen that the first identifiable victims of capital punishment in this country suffered death by beheading. The method of execution most associated with Britain though, is hanging. The adoption of hanging, as the standard form of punishment for a wide range of offences, was a slow and gradual process, which began a few centuries after the end of the Roman occupation in the fifth century AD.

The first recorded instances of hanging as a judicial punishment in this country are to be found during the Anglo-Saxon period, which immediately preceded the Norman Conquest in 1066. Generally though, during the periods when the Anglo-Saxons and Vikings ruled much of this country, executions were rare. An extensive system of financial compensation was the norm instead. Every injury, from a lost eye to the murder of a husband, could be calculated in monetary terms; the criminal simply paid the victim or his relatives the appropriate sum in silver or gold. Alfred the Great set out a complete scale of compensation to be paid for various offences – starting with the loss of a tooth and going all the way up to the murder of an Archbishop. This changed after the arrival of the Normans. It was William the Conqueror's youngest son, William Rufus, who made hanging a standard punishment in England. It was at first laid down as the penalty not for murder, but for poaching Royal deer. William Rufus' brother Henry, who became King Henry I on the death of his brother in 1100, really began the wholesale use of hanging as a judicial punishment in Britain. During his reign, hanging became the accepted punishment for a wide range of offences, ranging from theft to murder.

Why this enthusiasm for hanging, combined with mutilations such as the removal of eyes and hands? The answer is simple. In Britain today, we rely upon a complicated and expensive nationwide system for the detection and punishment of crime. Prisons for example, cost a great deal to run and are funded by central government from money raised by taxes. The idea of paying to feed and house a criminal, for years at a time, would have seemed utterly bizarre to a Norman baron. Some of the money which he raised from his tenants would have been sent to the King in London, but otherwise, he was free to hang on to as much as he could. Why would he use this money to feed and house poachers, rebels, outlaws and thieves who threatened the smooth running of his district? Hanging or beheading a man disposed of the problem quickly and neatly, with little expense. For lesser offences, cutting off a man's hand would ensure that if he was caught again, it would be obvious that this was a second offence and thus justified inflicting the death penalty. Branding sometimes served the same purpose. As well as identifying repeat offenders, these measures were also intended to act as deterrents in themselves.

The great advantage of hanging from the point of view of a pre-industrial society, as opposed to other methods of execution, is that requires no special equipment, nor any particular skill on the part of the executioner. In its simplest form, all that is needed is a length of rope and a convenient tree. Once the condemned man has been tied up, all that is necessary is to throw the rope over a branch, tie it round the neck of the victim and then haul him into the air to strangle. This, indeed, is how most hangings were carried out in the years following the Norman Conquest. It was not long though, before various refinements were developed. For one thing, it was thought necessary to conduct executions, for their deterrent effect, in cities and towns. For this purpose, it was found more convenient to erect a wooden framework, both to make the suspension of the felon easier, but also to ensure that his death throes could be more easily seen by the large crowds who gathered for such events. This was, of course, the origin of the gallows. These early gallows were little more than upright wooden posts linked by a crosspiece. There was no sort of mechanism – that came a good deal later. The rope would be of such a length as to suspend the criminal a good way from the ground and they would be made to climb a ladder propped up against the gallows. The noose would be secured and the ladder simply twisted in order to precipitate the condemned man or woman into eternity. One explanation for the superstitious belief that walking beneath a ladder is unlucky dates from these primitive hangings. Walking beneath the ladder was the last thing which a condemned man did before his death. Unlucky indeed! Even after the introduction of custom-built frameworks, trees continued to be used for hanging well into the eighteenth century. The execution of Mary Blandy, at Oxford in 1752, was accomplished by wedging a stout piece of timber between two adjacent trees and hanging the woman from this.

I said earlier that executions were conducted in towns and villages, but this is not strictly accurate. It would be more correct to say that they were carried out on the edges of towns. For the full, deterrent effect, one wanted as many spectators as possible, and this meant that the narrow streets of a medieval town might not accommodate them all. On the other hand, there is no point in stringing up a man in some remote spot, miles from any human habitation. The most popular spot for the gallows was therefore just outside a town, where there was plenty of room for the crowds to gather, in a place that could easily be accessed on foot. It was this reasoning which led to the establishment of perhaps the most famous gallows of all, that of Tyburn, which was erected on the outskirts of London.

Deaths from hanging of this sort almost invariably resulted from strangulation, rather than the clean breaking of the neck, which became the aim of hanging in the late nineteenth century. Strangling to death on the end of a rope is a slow and distressing business. Death can take up to half an hour and, until the loss of consciousness, the victim suffers appallingly. Reflexive voiding of urine almost invariably occurs, which gave rise to a number of coarse sayings in connection with hanging; for example, 'A man will piss when he cannot whistle' and also, 'There's no more to a hanging than a wry neck and a wet pair of breeches.'

Death on the gallows through slow strangulation might have been hideous, but it provided a tiny spark of hope to those undergoing it. This was the chance that a person might, under some circumstances, survive the operation. We shall in later chapters see examples of this, but we look now at the earliest recorded account of this phenomenon, that of the Welsh rebel, William Cragh.

In the late thirteenth century, Edward I fought various campaigns against the Welsh, who were opposed to English rule of their country. One of those who was captured, after some bitter fighting, was William Cragh (also known as William the Scabby and William ap Rhys). He was accused of killing thirteen men and after a brief trial, was sentenced to hang. On the morning of Monday, 27 November 1290, Cragh and another man were hanged side by side, their bodies being left on the gallows until four o'clock that afternoon. For some unknown reason, the wife of a local nobleman requested that she be allowed to bury the young rebel, and Cragh's corpse was accordingly delivered to her home in Swansea.

We have the son of the woman who asked for William Cragh's body to thank for the vivid description of the dead man. Writing some years later, William de Briouze painted the scene graphically:

His face was black and in parts bloody or stained with blood. His eyes had come out of their sockets and hung outside the eyelids and the sockets were filled with blood. His mouth, neck, and throat and the parts around them, and also his nostrils, were filled with blood, so that it was impossible in the natural course of things for him to breathe. His tongue hung out of his mouth, the length of a man's finger, and it was completely black and swollen and as thick with the blood sticking to it that it seemed the size of a man's two fists together

William Cragh had also, in his final extremity, emptied both his bladder and bowels. There seemed little doubt that he had died the usual, agonising death of anybody who had been hanged. Nevertheless, Lady Mary de Briouze prayed to Thomas de Cantilupe, the former bishop of Hereford, who had recently died. The day after his hanging, William Cragh showed some signs of life; within a fortnight he was as healthy as anybody else, and apparently none the worse for his execution.

This seeming miracle was investigated in detail by a commission from Rome, who were trying to establish whether or not Thomas de Cantilupe should be canonised. They concluded that William Cragh had actually been killed and raised from the dead by the prayers to the dead bishop, who was later declared a saint.

What had really happened, of course, was that Cragh had simply survived his hanging, something which happened from time to time. Sometimes the victim was especially light; on other occasions the knot was too stiff to pull tight and choke the hanging person. It was also not unknown for the body to be cut down before life was wholly extinct.

Hanging flourished in Britain in the following years, reaching a crescendo during the reign of Henry VIII. According to some estimates, more than 72,000 people were put to death while Henry was king, which works out at almost 2,000 executions a year, over the course of the thirty-eight years that he was on the throne. The vast majority of these executions would have been by hanging. At this time, the death penalty was not restricted to serious crimes such as murder, but could be imposed for such trifling matters as stealing birds' eggs or associating with Gypsies. It was often the case that more than one person would be hanged at a time during the Tudor years. The authorities waited until a reasonable number of prisoners were being held under sentence of death, and then hanged them all simultaneously. The sight of a dozen or more men and women choking to death on the end of ropes was thought to be more impressive than one or two.

In 1571, a novel type of gallows was erected in the village of Tyburn, which in Tudor times was some way west of the city of London and Westminster. Tyburn was roughly where the modern-day districts of Paddington and

Marble Arch are to be found. It was first recorded as being a site for hanging in the twelfth century, when Williams Fitz Osbern led a rebellion. He was dragged naked to the edge of the Tyburn stream and hanged there. From that time onwards, the hanging of those sentenced to death in London was usually carried out on this spot, although executions also took place at Tower Hill and other locations closer to the City of London.

The new gallows were a permanent structure, which stood right in the middle of the road leading into London from the west. Most gallows consisted of two uprights with a crossbar. The one at Tyburn was made of a large equilateral wooden triangle, which was supported on three posts. Half a dozen or more people could be hanged from each of the three crossbars. The record on this gallows, a record not just for Tyburn but for the entire country, was twenty-three men and one woman, all hanged together on 23 June 1649.

It may seem odd to us today to think of a gallows being erected in the middle of a main road, but there was a reason for this apparently bizarre arrangement. In the first place, we must bear in mind that the traffic, along even a main road in Tudor times, would not be anything like the rate of flow of cars along a busy road today. It would, instead, consist in the main of pedestrians, riders and the occasional carriage or cart. The new gallows would impede the flow of traffic no more than a modern roundabout. Siting it in the middle of the road was done in order to fulfil what was then seen as the main purpose of capital punishment – to be a very public deterrent.

There is an apocryphal story, from about this time, which neatly sums up the attitude which many ordinary people had towards executions in general and hangings in particular. A shipwrecked sailor staggered ashore in an unknown country. The first thing he saw was a gallows standing stark upon a nearby hill. 'Thank God,' he supposedly cried, 'I am in a civilised land.' This tale illustrates the very different point of view to be found in Britain three or four centuries ago. The public gallows showed that law and order were enforced. It was as reassuring a sight as a Bobby on the beat might have been a generation ago. Gallows and gibbets, similar structures whose purpose was to preserve and display the remains of a hanged man, were to be seen all over the country. To this day, many districts have places named Gallows Corner or Gibbet Hill. The gallows and gibbet were landmarks, a constant reminder to those who passed them that this was a country where law and order were valued and rigorously enforced.

Placing the new permanent gallows at Tyburn, on the main road into London from the west, acted as perfect counterpoint for the gateway above London Bridge; the only point of entry to London from the south, with its ghastly forest of spikes, each topped with the head of an executed man. The message to travellers, in both cases, was clear and quite unambiguous. Here was a city which was quick to punish criminals and wrongdoers.

The gallows at Tyburn became a London institution. Hangings still took place at other locations in the city, but Tyburn was the big event. Hangings there took on the characteristics of a fairground. The crowds on hanging days were immense and a whole tribe of tradesman grew up to service the spectators' needs. Snacks and drinks were on sale and stands were set up – much like those from which we watch sporting events today. Copies of supposed confessions of those to be hanged were hawked, while the whole area took on the appearance of a football ground at the time of a Cup Final. There was an almost unbelievable callousness about the whole business of executing a dozen or more men and women, guilty, in many cases, of nothing more than the theft of a few pennies' worth of goods.

The gallows at Tyburn became known by a number of imaginative names – the triple tree, the three-legged mare, the never-green tree. Its fame spread far beyond the London area, as did the figures of speech and folklore associated with it. Those travelling from the city to be hanged at Tyburn were literally 'going west' – an expression still in use today to indicate the end of some project. This familiarity with hanging led, perhaps inevitably, to a situation where the solemnity and awe of being in the presence of death became replaced with ribald revelry. In short, what was supposed to act as a deterrent became, instead, part of the backdrop of everyday life. Ministers who spoke to condemned criminals discovered that almost every one of them had witnessed hangings themselves, without it having any noticeable effect upon their future conduct or way of life.

These public hangings eventually led to the development of a more humane and scientific method of execution. It was noticed that some people 'died hard', that is to say kicking and struggling on the end of the rope, while others seemed to die at once. This was seen during the execution of the men who had been convicted of the Gunpowder Plot, in 1606. Guy Fawkes and seven other men had been sentenced to be hanged, drawn and quartered for their attempt to blow up the king and Parliament buildings. The idea was that all the men would be hanged for a short while, and then butchered while still alive and conscious. All the conspirators, bar Fawkes himself, were castrated and disembowelled while alive and fully conscious. When the time came for Guy Fawkes to mount the ladder, he did so slowly and painfully, as he had been tortured during his interrogation in the Tower of London. At the final moment though, he somehow found a last reserve of strength and leaped from the ladder. The drop broke his neck and he died instantly; the only member of the conspiracy to escape the horrors of being dismembered alive.

Up until the late eighteenth century, some condemned men and women took this opportunity to try and end their agony as swiftly as possible. This was easier when horses and cart began to be used for simultaneous group hangings. Many such mass executions had at least one victim jumping from the cart voluntarily, before the horses were whipped into action. James Maclean, a highwayman, took this option when he was about to be hanged at Tyburn on 3 October 1750. Once the rope had been placed around his neck and the cart was about to move off, he kicked off his shoes and leapt high into the air, drawing his knees up to his chest as he did so. He fell like a plummet, his neck snapping instantly.

On the other hand, of course, those who simply submitted to the usual type of hanging had a very slight chance of surviving their execution. We saw one example of this earlier in this chapter and this might be an appropriate point at which to consider another, even better authenticated example, of this phenomenon.

In 1723, Margaret Dickson was living with her husband and two children in Musselburgh, a village near Edinburgh. She fell out with her husband and left him, setting off on foot to stay with her aunt in Newcastle. En route, she managed to get a job at an inn in Maxwellheugh, another village in the Edinburgh area. There is some doubt as to the precise sequence of events, but it is agreed that she became pregnant by either her employer or one of his sons. She kept quiet about the pregnancy, and the first that anybody knew of the matter was the discovery of the body of a newborn baby floating in the nearby river Tweed. Evidence led to Margaret Dickson and she soon found herself on trial for her life.

Margaret was charged with the murder of her child. Her story was that the baby had been stillborn and that she had disposed of it in the river. This seemed such a callous and unfeeling way of dealing with a loss of this sort, that it probably prejudiced the jury against her. She was, at any rate, found guilty and sentenced to hang at Grassmarket in Edinburgh on 24 September 1724. Thousands turned up for the execution, which was uneventful. She was suspended from the gallows for over half an hour, and the hangman even hung from her legs for a while to ensure that she was dead. Margaret Dickson's body was placed in a plain wooden coffin and her family set out on the 6 mile walk to Musselburgh, in order to bury her in her home town. So far, so good and there was nothing to distinguish this from the many thousands of similar executions carried out during the eighteenth century.

The funeral party stopped at an alehouse for refreshments, and it was then that a scratching was heard from inside the coffin. It was opened and Margaret Dickson was found to be alive. She went on to live for many more years.

We have seen that within a century or so of the Norman invasion, hanging had become the standard method for inflicting death upon criminals. Beheading was, as a rule, reserved for those of noble birth and burning for heretics and some women convicted of treason. The punishment of hanging, drawing and quartering, which we will look at in detail in Chapter 7, was reserved for commoners found guilty of treason. It was thought indecent to expose to public sight the naked bodies of women found guilty of this offence, and so it was 'commuted' to burning. All these types of executions amounted to a handful of exceptional and atypical cases; perhaps 99 per cent of executions in Britain have been by hanging, certainly for the last 1,000 years or so.

As Britain entered the eighteenth century, hanging had become the standard response to any number of crimes. Today, we are used to the idea that the death penalty should be reserved for particularly serious crimes such as murder, but this was not the way of thinking a few centuries ago. The number of offences carrying the death penalty increased year by year, reaching a zenith with the Bloody Code, which remained in force until the early nineteenth century. We shall look at this period, which can aptly be described as the heyday of British hanging, in Chapter 6. Firstly, I want first to look at the curious case of mechanical devices for removing heads; two examples of which were to be found in Britain long before the invention of the guillotine.

MECHANICAL DECAPITATION: A BRITISH INVENTION

It is an enduring image of France: the triangular blade of the guillotine speeding down towards the neck of some luckless victim. It evokes the memory of Dickens' *A Tale of Two Cities* or perhaps *The Scarlet Pimpernel*. However, the guillotine was not a French invention at all, it was a British one. Such devices were in use in this country for centuries before the French Revolution, and versions of them were to be found in two major British cities.

Many of us are familiar with the so-called Beggars' or Thieves' Litany, 'From Hell, Hull and Halifax, Good Lord deliver us'. It is easy enough to see why one would wish to be saved from Hell, but why Halifax and Hull? This little jingle dates from the early seventeenth century and Hull, at that time, had a notoriously harsh prison. It is Halifax which is of interest to us though, because here, at Halifax, was the prototype for the guillotine, which had been operating in that city since the thirteenth century. It was this device and the circumstances under which it was used, which caused Halifax to be included in the Beggars' Litany. In fact, the next verse of this poem, written by John Taylor and published in 1622, makes everything clear. It says:

At Halifax, the Law so sharp doth deal,
That whoso more than thirteen pence doth steal,
They have a jyn that wondrous quick and well
Sends Thieves all headless unto Heav'n or Hell
(Jyn is short for engine)

We saw earlier that a tradition had grown up in this country, by which only those of noble or royal blood were executed by beheading. For the ordinary murderer or thief, hanging was thought to be the proper mode of execution. In the English town of Halifax and also in Edinburgh, the Scottish capital, things were a little different. Let us look first at Halifax, where the first recorded machine for human decapitation was once to be found.

Halifax is in the county of Yorkshire and has, for centuries, been associated with the production of fabrics and clothing. Even today, the nearby towns of Leeds and Bradford still maintain their connection to the textiles industry. The manufacture of woollen cloth in Halifax dates back to at least the medieval period. There are indirect allusions to the industry there from around AD 1150. The reason for this is that the soil in this area is not very fertile and the town needed to find another source of income, besides farming. An industry based upon sheep farming, common elsewhere in the county, fitted the bill perfectly.

In 1286 the manorial court of the area, which included the town of Halifax, was granted the right to execute anybody found guilty of stealing woollen cloth. This became known as the Halifax Gibbet Law. It was in this year that the first person was supposedly executed by means of the 'Halifax Gibbet'. The Halifax Gibbet was, in fact, the prototype for all mechanical devices for decapitating people.

We do not know who invented the Halifax Gibbet, although legends exist about its origins. A long ballad by Thomas Deloney called 'Thomas of Reading', contains a detailed account of the supposed circumstances which led to the construction of the gibbet. The poem, published in 1600, tells of a group of local clothiers who obtained permission from the Crown to execute those who stole cloth in this area. Unfortunately, nobody was prepared to act as hangman, this being a post which was traditionally of very low status. A travelling friar arrived in the town and devised a machine which would take off the heads of 'valiant rogues', without anybody having to be solely responsible for the act. In other words, executions could take place without anybody getting their hands dirty. This was because of the way that the gibbet was made; it meant that everybody present would take hold of the rope which released the blade and no one person could be said to be responsible.

In appearance, the Halifax Gibbet looked almost exactly like the guillotine. Two tall uprights were capped with a crossbar. At the base was a semi-circular hole in which the victim's neck could lay snugly. A heavy block of wood, with a metal blade attached to it, slid up and down and could be hoisted to the top of the uprights and then secured in position with a pin. The condemned man knelt and placed his head beneath the blade, which was then released. Its mode of operation was thus precisely similar to that of the later French guillotine. There were two minor differences, one of which was very significant and allowed at least several people to escape execution at the last moment.

The most obvious difference between the Halifax Gibbet and the guillotine was in the design of the blade. The blade of the guillotine was set at an angle, giving it the appearance of a triangle, whereas that of the Halifax Gibbet was, in effect, a standard, crescent-shaped axe blade, which was embedded in a stout block of wood. This, in turn, was surmounted by a mass of lead to increase its weight and effectiveness. Although this seemed to accomplish the job well enough (there are no references in history to anybody's head not being severed at once), it was probably not as neat and surgical an operation as when Madame Guillotine went to work. There is reason to suppose that heads removed by this method was more squashed off at the neck, rather than being cleanly cut, as was the case with the guillotine.

Although we are all familiar with the final version of the guillotine, with its iconic, angled blade, the first prototypes lacked this refinement. A German harpsichord maker, called Tobias Schmidt, constructed the first French beheading machine in 1791. He used an ordinary axe blade at first, but this proved not to be up to the job. The new machine decapitated a number of live sheep successfully and then two human corpses. The third corpse to be tested had tough neck muscles, and it took three attempts to sever the head. There is a story that King Louis XVI, a keen amateur locksmith, suggested the refinement of having the blade set at an acute angle. If true, this would have been ironic in the extreme, as he was later to become one of the most famous victims of this new method of execution.

The other difference between both the Halifax Gibbet and the Scottish 'Maiden' (which we will discuss later), as opposed to the guillotine, was that there was no board on which to strap the condemned person. It was necessary, with both British devices, to kneel and place the head voluntarily in the correct place, just as though being beheaded with an axe and block.

Before we go any further, let us read an account of the operation of the Halifax Gibbet by a Tudor historian, Raphael Holinshed. He was the source for many of the stories which Shakespeare adapted for his plays. His reliability in matters of ancient history may sometimes be a little dubious, but in this case he was writing about what was actually happening at that time in his own country. It is probably safe to take his evidence as being sound:

Witches are hanged or sometimes burned, but thieves are hanged . . . generally on the gibbet or gallows, saving in Halifax where they are beheaded after a strange manner, and whereof I find this report. There is and hath been of ancient time a law or rather a custom at Halifax, that who so ever doth commit any felony, and is taken with the same, or confess the fact upon examination; if it be valued by four constables to amount to the sum of thirteen pence half penny, he is forthwith beheaded upon one of the next market days (which fall usually upon the Tuesdays, Thursdays, and Saturdays) or else upon the same day that he is so convicted, if market then be held. The engine wherewith the execution is done, is a square block of wood of the length of fourfoot and a half, which doth ride by and down in a slot between two pieces of timber, that are framed and set upright of five yards in height. In the nether end of the sliding block is an axe keyed or fastened with an iron into the wood, which being drawn up to the top of the frame is there fastened by a wooden pin (with a notch made into the same after the manner of a Sampson post) into the middle of which pin also there is a long rope fastened that cometh down among the people, so that when the offender hath made his confession, and hath laid his neck over the nethermost block, every man there present doth either take hold of the rope (or puts forth his arm so near to the same as he can get, in token that he is willing to see true justice executed) and pulling out the pin in this manner, the head block wherein the axe is fastened doth fall down with such violence, that if the neck of the transgressor were so big as that of a bull, it should be cut in sunder at a stroke, and roll from the body by an huge distance. If it be so that the offender be apprehended for an ox, oxen, sheep, horse, or any such cattle; the self beast or other of the same kind shall have the end of the rope tied somewhere unto them, so that they being driven do draw out the pin whereby the offender is executed. Thus much of Halifax law, which I set down only to show the custom of that country in this behalf.

There are several noteworthy features about this description. There was the curious custom that if a man stole an animal, such as a horse or cow, then the animal itself would carry out the execution by pulling out the pin which released the blade. This is a procedure surely unique in the story of British capital punishment. Another interesting point is the participation of all citizens in the process; everybody pulling, or at the very least signifying their willingness to pull, the rope which brought down the blade. This obviated the need for an executioner, and showed that all the citizens approved of what was being done.

Holinshed notes another unique feature of executions by the Halifax Gibbet. He says, 'so that when the offender hath made his confession, and hath laid his neck over the nethermost block.' This sounds like some minor detail of Elizabethan religious observance. The priest heard his confession before the man was executed. So what? we are tempted to ask. Wasn't that common enough during executions in those days? In fact, this is not at all what is being talked of here. Holinshed is referring to yet another unique custom associated with capital punishment in Halifax; no criminal could be executed unless he had confessed his crime and acknowledged that the sentence was just. In the late eighteenth century, a writer in Halifax confirmed that this had been the case, saying:

If upon examination they do find that the said felon is not only guilty of the goods stolen, and lying, or being in their view, but also do find the value of the goods stolen, to be of thirteen pence halfpenny or above, then is the felon found guilty by the said jury; grounding that their verdict upon the evidence of the goods stolen and lying before them, together with his own confession, which, in such cases, is always required; and being so found guilty, is by them condemned to be beheaded, according to ancient custom.

One is at a loss to know why the accused should confess to the crime, knowing that failure to do so would save him from having his head chopped off! It is hard to avoid the suspicion that a certain amount of persuasion, possibly in the form of torture, must have been applied in order to deliver the required outcome. It has been suggested that the fear of perjuring oneself, in those days, would have been greater than the terror of being beheaded. Telling lies under an oath sworn to God would, at least in theory, have been enough to place one's immortal soul in jeopardy, and this could perhaps have made an honest confession more likely. An explanation for this strange situation is that the requirement for confession to precede execution was only applicable in cases where the thief had not been directly apprehended in the act of stealing. Since there were no detectives in those days, this was probably the only category of criminal convicted. If they were not caught red-handed, then they probably got away with it.

It is possible that Holinshed is mistaken about the law relating to any goods over the value of 13*d*. The probability is that these executions were restricted either to the theft of cloth or livestock. Writing less than a century after the last execution by the Halifax Gibbet, Daniel Defoe, author of *Robinson Crusoe*, wrote that:

I must not quit Halifax till I give you some account of the famous course of justice anciently executed here, to prevent the stealing of cloth. Modern accounts pretend to say it was for all sorts of felonies, but I am well assured it was first erected purely, or at least principally, for such thieves as were apprehended stealing cloth from the tenters; and it seems very reasonable to think it was so, because of the conditions of the trial.

The mention of 'tenters' requires a little explanation. Tenters are frames on which material or cloth, which has recently been woven, is hung. When the textiles trade first came to be established in this part of Yorkshire, it was important that those carrying out the work could simply leave the tenters out with the material on them. Any interference with the apparatus of the textile industry touched upon the prosperity of the whole town, and that is why the penalties were so severe.

We know other things about the gibbet, things which are not mentioned in old writings. For instance, we know that it stood on a stone platform which was 4ft high and about 12ft long. How do we know this? Simply because the platform is still there. After the last beheading, undertaken by the Halifax Gibbet in 1650, the machine itself was dismantled and put into storage. The blade has survived and may be seen today in the Bankfield Museum, in Boothtown, Halifax. The platform upon which it stood was neglected and overgrown, eventually becoming a rubbish dump, whose local name, Gibbet Hill, gave a clue as to its origins. When the site was being cleared, before a warehouse was built there in June 1839, the original stone platform was uncovered, hidden beneath a couple of centuries of rubbish. Buried nearby were two headless skeletons, which were presumed to be the remains of the last two men to be dealt with by the old gibbet.

We come now to a 'Get out of jail free' card. If, after the blade had been released, the prisoner could pull his head free of the gibbet and then escape from the area; then he had to be allowed to go free. Specifically, he had to get clear of the 'Liberty' or legal district where the Halifax Gibbet Law was in force. This stretched for 10 miles to the west and 1 mile to the south. The northern edge of the liberty was only a few hundred paces of the gibbet. Once beyond this boundary, there was no legal method for compelling the escaped offender to return. As long as he stayed clear of the Halifax liberty for the rest of his life, he was home and dry. Two cases illustrate how this worked in practice.

In the early part of the seventeenth century, a man called Dinnis was due to be beheaded. He had been found guilty and confessed. On the appointed market day, he was led up the steps to the gibbet and knelt submissively, placing his head beneath the raised blade. By strange tradition, a bagpiper played a lament during executions in Halifax. As he heard the pin being removed, Dinnis whipped back his head and made a run for it. He headed north and encountered sightseers heading towards his execution. Somebody asked him if Dinnis was to be beheaded that day. The fleeing man replied dryly, 'I trow not' (I think not). 'I trow not' became a proverb locally, which is still used in that part of Yorkshire to indicate that some event is unlikely to take place.

As far as we know, Dinnis was wise enough to keep going and never return to Halifax. In 1617, John Lacey achieved a similar escape, getting clear of the liberty and remaining free for seven years, until 1623. He then made the foolish mistake of returning to Halifax, labouring under the misapprehension that his escape had nullified the sentence passed against him. He soon learnt that this was not the case, being seized and executed by the gibbet without any further need for a trial. There is a public house in Halifax called The Running Man, which celebrates John Lacey's escape.

Although the Halifax Gibbet was a far cruder machine that the guillotine and lacked many of that instrument's refinements, it certainly managed to do the job of removing heads from bodies well enough. True, the guillotine was an incomparably finer piece of work; as well it might be, having been built by a harpsichord maker. Spirit levels were used when erecting it for use, to ensure that the blade fell smoothly, and there were any number of other aspects which made the Halifax Gibbet look crude by comparison. Still, it accomplished its purpose very well, as a number of anecdotes confirm.

When the guillotine removed somebody's head, the head dropped neatly into a little basket placed ready to receive it. This was not the case with the Halifax Gibbet. Either because the blade was a little blunt or because of its design, which relied more on brute force than the angled and bevelled blade of the guillotine, the blade used in the Halifax Gibbet took off a head with a good deal of force. The momentum imparted to decapitated heads by this primitive device could be considerable. Not to put to fine a point on it, the heads shot a considerable distance from the site of the execution. There is a story of a woman riding through the market on an execution day. When the blade of the gibbet fell, the head was propelled through the air and actually landed in the woman's lap. She was presumably riding side-saddle. Not only did the head strike her, but the teeth, perhaps by reflex muscular action, gripped her clothes with such force that there was some difficulty in removing the ghastly object from her lap. Another anecdote tells of a head being hurled into the air, before landing neatly in somebody's basket.

There is some reason to suppose that the Halifax Gibbet was not the only beheading machine operating in Yorkshire during the Middle Ages. It was certainly the last to be used, and has, perhaps, become famous because of this. The Halifax Gibbet was not used as frequently as the gallows were in other districts. The records show that between 1541 and 1650, only fifty-three people were executed by it in total. This averages out at one victim every two years. The final executions were both conducted on the same day in April 1650. These two men, John Wilkinson and Anthony Mitchell, both from Sowerby, had been convicted of theft. Between them, they had stolen sixteen yards of material belonging to Samuel Colbeck of Warley; the material being valued at 1s a yard. They had also made off with two colts belonging to John Cusforth, who lived near Wakefield. Mitchell was also found guilty of stealing another piece of cloth.

Why was the use of the Halifax Gibbet discontinued? It has been suggested that this might have been in reaction to the beheading of Charles I, the previous year. It is thought that the act of cutting off a king's head made this type of execution generally unpopular. This is, however, only speculation. We do not know why such an apparently effective deterrent should have been so abruptly abandoned.

As far as is known, the Halifax Gibbet was the first beheading machine ever devised, although there are rumours that something of the sort was being used in Ireland centuries earlier. The only information on this machine though, dates from the sixteenth century. A picture from that period exists, it is called, 'The execution of Murcod Ballagh near to Merton in Ireland 1307'. This shows a machine almost identical in appearance to the Halifax Gibbet. Whether the artist simply copied a picture of the Halifax Gibbet, or whether this is an authentic and different device, is impossible to say now.

That a decapitation machine existed before either the guillotine or the Halifax Gibbet is undeniable, and it is quite possible that both these later devices were based upon the Italian mannaia. Its first recorded use was on 29 October 1268, when it was used to remove the head of Conradin Hohenstaufen of Swabia. Writing much later, a Dominican priest called Jean-Baptist Labat describes the mannaia as it was operating in 1730. It had two uprights holding a blade which was 10in across, which weighed about 80lbs. This machine certainly inspired the guillotine, but whether an earlier version was the prototype for the Halifax Gibbet, or whether it was itself a copy of the English mechanism, is impossible to say.

A device very similar to the Halifax Gibbet was certainly operating in Edinburgh from the sixteenth century onwards, but this was no more than a copy of the English machine. In 1563, James Douglas, 4th Earl of Morton, was appointed Lord Chancellor of Scotland and that same year he visited Yorkshire where, it is supposed, he saw the Halifax Gibbet in action. He was so impressed with the speed and ease with which criminals could be executed in this way, that when he returned to Scotland, he commissioned a copy of the Halifax Gibbet to be used in Edinburgh.

The Scottish machine featured one important improvement, which was a hinged iron bar clamping the victim's neck in place during the execution. There would be no question of any condemned man in Edinburgh jerking his head out of the way at the last moment! There is an old piece of folk etymology which suggests that the Scottish machine was christened the 'maiden' because it took a long time for it to see any action. This is not true, although it was two years before it was first used. In fact, 'maiden', in this sense, is a corruption of the Gaelic 'modrun', which is a term used for a place of judgement.

One story suggests that the Earl of Morton had a model of the Halifax Gibbet made while he was visiting the north of England, and that those who built the maiden copied the model. This seems unlikely, especially in view of the modification of the iron restraining bar for the neck. We know, at any rate, who constructed the Edinburgh maiden. Two carpenters called Adam and Patrick Shang made the framework, and a man called Andrew Gotterson helped with the blade. The Shangs were furniture makers and had made a bed for Mary Queen of Scots' brother. Perhaps this is how they got the commission for building the maiden, since Mary was on the throne of Scotland at the time. They were paid 40s for their work on the maiden.

The first person to die beneath the maiden's blade was Thomas Scott. He had been part of a group of men who stabbed to death David Rizzio, the Queen's private secretary and, it was widely rumoured, her lover. Rizzio's body was left with fifty-seven wounds. On 3 April 1566, Scott and his fellow assassins were beheaded. The maiden claimed 150 lives until it was retired in 1708. Perhaps the most surprising victim of Scotland's answer to the guillotine was the man who had been responsible for introducing this novel means of execution. In 1581, the Earl of Morton, one-time regent, was accused of complicity in the murder of Mary Queen of Scots' husband, Lord Darnley. Following a brief trial, he was conducted to the City Cross and beheaded by the very machine whose use he had championed.

The maiden seems, like the Halifax Gibbet and the French guillotine, to have been a completely egalitarian means of execution. Commoners and nobles alike died beneath its blade. Following the restoration of the monarchy in 1660, a number of Scots who had sided with Parliament during the Civil War were put on trial. Among these was Archibald Campbell, 1st Marquess of Argyle. On 21 May 1661, he was beheaded by the maiden in Edinburgh; his head was displayed on a spike over one of the city gates. Twenty-five years later, his son raised an army in support of Monmouth's rising in the west country of England. He too was convicted of treason and, like his father, was beheaded in the same way.

The last person to be executed by the maiden is the subject of a legend, which could possibly be true. Sir Godfrey McCulloch was a landowner who had a long-running dispute with one of his neighbours – a William Gordon. So ferocious did the argument between the two men become, that it culminated with McCulloch shooting Gordon in the leg. The wound became infected and Gordon died, whereupon Sir Godfrey decamped to France in order to escape justice. This was in 1684. He remained in exile for thirteen years, but eventually returned to Scotland, perhaps hoping that the incident might have been forgotten by that time. It had not, and he attained immortality, of a kind, by being the last person to have his head removed by a mechanical device in Britain.

Although it was withdrawn from use in 1708 and put into storage, Lord Lovatt petitioned that the maiden should be used for his execution, rather than the English axe and block – a request which was denied. The maiden may be seen today in the National Museum of Scotland in Edinburgh.

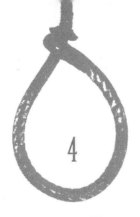

SHOT AT DAWN:
THE BRITISH FIRING SQUAD AT WORK

The glorious weather of Friday, 15 August 1941, must have been especially poignant to Josef Jakobs. A meteorologist by training, he had been seconded to the Wermacht's meteorological branch. At a little after seven o'clock on that fine summer morning, Sergeant Jakobs was about to earn a small footnote in history, by being the last person executed by a British firing squad, on British soil.

Earlier that year, Jakobs had parachuted into England wearing civilian clothes. Such an act, on the part of an enemy soldier during war, automatically merited the death penalty under British law. He landed near the town of Ramsey in Huntingdonshire on 31 January 1941. Among other things, Jakobs was equipped with £500 in cash, a loaded pistol and a short wave radio transmitter. His mission was to send information regarding British weather conditions back to Germany, thus allowing the German air force to time their bombing raids to their best advantage.

Unfortunately for Jakobs, he broke his ankle on jumping from the plane and injured it further on landing in a field on Dovehouse Farm. Since he couldn't walk, there was nothing for it but to summon help, which he did by firing his pistol into the air a few times. Charles Baldock and Harry Coulson, who were walking nearby at the time, came to the rescue. One stayed with the injured man while the other went for help. It was not long before Josef Jakobs was in the custody of the local Home Guard.

During his interrogation, it was revealed that Josef Jakobs had been born in Luxembourg in 1898. He claimed to have come to England in order to help fight the Nazis – an assertion which was treated with some scepticism by those questioning him. There is a mysterious gap of five months between Jakobs' capture and his interview by the police at Scotland Yard. It is thought that an attempt might have been made during this time to 'turn' him, and persuade him to act as a double-agent under the control of MI5. At any rate, it was not until 24 July that year that he was charged under Section I of the 1940 Treachery Act. Jakobs was very concerned as to what would happen to him if he were convicted of the charge. He asked the officer who read the charge to him, Lt-Col Cooke, whether he would be hanged or shot. Cooke explained that as a serving soldier himself, Jakobs would be tried by a court-martial, and in the case of his receiving the death penalty, it would be carried out by firing squad. The German seemed relieved to hear this. His trial took place at the Duke of York's HQ in Chelsea on the 4th and 5th of August.

The verdict of the court-martial was never seriously in doubt. The evidence was plain enough. Jakobs was a serving soldier in an enemy army who had chosen to put on civilian clothes and enter Britain illegally; he was accordingly sentenced to death.

A week after the trial, the Constable of the Tower of London received the following letter;

LD/SR A(s) 1 MOST SECRET
To: The Constable of H.M. Tower of London. 13th August 1941.

Sir,

I have the honour to acquaint you that JOSEF JAKOBS, an enemy alien, has been found guilty of an offence against the Treachery Act 1940 and has been sentenced to suffer death by being shot.
The said enemy alien has been attached to the Holding Battalion, Scots Guards for the purpose of punishment and the execution has been fixed to take place at H.M. Tower of London on Friday the 15th August 1941 at 7.15am.

Sgd. Sir Bertram N. Sergison-Brooke,
Lieutenant-General Commanding London District.

Preparations were made at the Tower of London for the execution. Tucked away in a dark alley behind the Constable Tower was a small-bore rifle range; the East Casemates Rifle Range. It was thought that this would be the most suitable location for the execution, because it was shielded from public view by the Tower's high external walls.

After he had been sentenced to death, Jakobs sent an appeal for mercy to George VI. It read:

The humble petition by Josef Jakobs, a prisoner under sentence of death.
To His Majesty the King.

May it please Your Majesty,

A most unhappy man makes this appeal for mercy at the hands of Your Majesty. On the 5th of August, 1941, Your Majesty's courts-martial condemned me to death, convinced that I came to Your Majesty' country with intent to cause her harm by transmitting information to the Nazis.

Your Majesty, in the face of death, I once again give the assurance which I have already given under oath before the courts-martial, I swear by dearest and most precious thing I possess, by the life of my three children that this never was and never could be the case, that it is just the opposite that I came to Your Majesty's country with the sole purpose of fighting on England's side against the Nazis. I came to Your Majesty's country with the sole purpose of joining in the fight for personal freedom, for religious freedom for my children, for freeing the German people from the frightful enslavement of the Nazi tyranny and not to die for the Nazi tyrants.

Your Majesty can obtain a clearer idea from the speech of my defending officer, Captain White, of the unfortunate circumstances of my landing, a landing which at the time, however, I considered fortunate. I have nothing to alter in his descriptions for they are entirely in accordance with the facts.

Should Your Majesty, however, believe that I am not worthy of Your Majesty's mercy, I beg Your Majesty to postpone the execution until the termination of the war, in order thereby to make it possible for me, at a fresh trial, to prove to the full my innocence by obtaining the attendance of witnesses now living in Germany and the production of documents. In the very nature of my case such evidence, which in fact exists, is by reason of the war not available to me. It is a difficulty which must face every enemy of the Nazis who leaves Germany and comes to this country. But surely England will not, for lack of such evidence, condemn to death a friend and one who will gladly help her.

Your Majesty, as the very facts of my arrival in this country will show Your Majesty, I am no coward I am not afraid of death. I would accept the verdict of the courts-martial without this appeal for mercy, if I felt myself even in the least guilty of the charge brought against me. But the opposite is the truth and for that reason I beg Your Majesty mercifully to refuse to confirm the sentence passed on me. A wife and three young children join with me in this appeal.

I do not want to close this appeal for mercy without assuring Your Majesty once again that Your Majesty would show mercy not to an enemy but to a friend, a true friend of England.

Your Majesty's most humble servant,
(sgd) Josef Jakobs.

And so it was that early on the morning of 15 August, Josef Jakobs, who was still unable to stand, due to the fact that his ankle had not healed properly, was seated in an ordinary chair at the end of the alleyway, which held the rifle range. A white-lint target was pinned over his heart, and an eight-man squad, consisting of soldiers from the Holding Battalion of the Scots Guards, took aim and, at the word of command, fired at the seated figure. Seven bullets smashed into his chest and the eighth went through his head. He died instantly.

Josef Jakobs was buried in an unmarked grave at St Mary's Roman Catholic cemetery at Kensal Green. He was not the last spy to be executed here during the Second World War, but as the others were civilians, they were hanged rather than shot. The chair in which Josef Jakobs was executed is still in the Tower of London. One of the back struts is splintered and broken; the bullets which passed through the executed man's heart carried straight on, smashing the chair and burying themselves in the wall of sandbags behind.

Execution by shooting is now the most popular and widespread form of capital punishment in the world. Countries as varied and disparate as Nigeria, Thailand, China and Cuba execute convicted criminals in this way. History does not record the origins of the firing squad as used in this country, but it probably has its roots in the practice of tying a man to a tree, and using him for archery practice. The ancient Britons certainly used bows and arrows for this purpose, prior to the Roman invasion of Britain. King Edmund the Martyr was killed in this way by the Vikings in around AD 870 – he was tied to a tree and used as a target by a group of bowmen.

Soldiers were being executed by gunfire in this country as early as the seventeenth century. A notorious case occurred following the siege of Colchester in 1648, during the English Civil War. The town was held by the Royalists and the Parliamentarians, under General Fairfax, found it a long and arduous task to break through the fortified positions. Eventually, the defenders surrendered. Fairfax pardoned all the rank-and-file, but decided to make an example of the four Royalist commanders. Sir George Lisle, Sir Charles Lucas, Colonel Farr and Bernard Gascoigne were all sentenced to death at a drumhead court-martial. Gascoigne was reprieved because he was a foreign national, while Farr managed to escape. The other two men were shot by a firing squad in the grounds of Colchester Castle, on the evening of 28 August 1648. An obelisk now marks the spot where the so-called Royalist Martyrs met their death.

From the beginning, the firing squad was recognised in Britain as being primarily a military punishment. Honourable death by powder and lead was regarded as a perfectly respectable way to go; almost on a par with falling on the battlefield. It was a soldier's death. This explains Jakobs' anxiety on being captured as to the mode of his death, if convicted of the charge against him. In this country especially, there was traditionally a hierarchy of judicial death. At the very top were executions by beheading. These were reserved for the aristocracy or even, as we saw in Chapter 2, for royalty themselves. Slightly below this came death by shooting, always provided that it was conducted by a firing squad. Hanging came at the bottom of the league, with the sub-division of hanging, drawing and quartering (which we shall look in Chapter 7) being the lowest type of death of all.

The purpose of having a squad of men to administer death by shooting is twofold. In the first instance, it spreads responsibility for the death among eight or ten people, thus lessening the guilt of each individual. This idea was extended in the twentieth century by the inclusion of a blank cartridge in one of the rifles; so allowing each member of the firing squad to believe that it was not his shot which contributed to the victim's death. This practice became very common, with the rifles being loaded and then shuffled around a little, so that nobody could tell which was which. Anybody who has actually fired a military rifle will know that the kick to the shoulder caused by the recoil of firing a live round of ammunition is quite different from the sensation of firing a blank cartridge. This particular little subterfuge is unlikely to have fooled any member of a firing party.

The other purpose of using a group of individuals, rather than one person, is that it enables the death to be removed a little further, by having the condemned man placed twenty-five yards away rather than being right next to the executioners. Putting the man at this distance and placing a target over his heart has the effect of dehumanising him and turning him into an object – a target, rather than a person.

In Soviet Russia, executions by shooting entailed the executioner placing a pistol against the back of the victim's neck. Shooting a man in this way is the most intimate form of execution imaginable, with killer and victim almost embracing. Aiming at a target at the other end of a rifle range, on the other hand, makes it possible to get out of one's mind the unpalatable thought that one is doing to death a fellow being.

One of the earliest detailed accounts of an execution by shooting in Britain dates from 1743. In May of that year there was unrest in Scotland, which was to culminate in the uprising of 1745. This was connected with the Scottish disputes between the Hanoverian monarchs of Britain and the Stuart pretenders to the Throne, who enjoyed great support in the Highlands. One of the Highland regiments, the Black Watch, had been ordered to London so that they could be reviewed by King George II. Once they reached the outskirts of London and were camped near Highgate, a rumour began to circulate that the summons to London was a trick, and that their loyalty to the House of Hanover had been questioned. The story, as it quickly spread, was that the entire regiment was to be shipped off to America and would never see their homes again. About a hundred of the men decided to return to Scotland at once.

This was a very orderly and peaceful mutiny. The men formed up in good order, under the control of two corporals, and marched in military style north towards Scotland. They were intercepted en route and agreed to surrender their arms and return to the capital. They were brought to London and lodged in the Tower. It was decided to make an example of the ringleaders, three of whom were tried for mutiny and sentenced to death. They were the two corporals, Farquhar Shaw and Samuel Macpherson and a private, Malcolm Macpherson.

The executions took place, in keeping with custom, at first light on 19 July 1743. The other mutineers were assembled by Tower Green to witness the event. The three condemned men were led out, and then told to kneel in front of a wall of the chapel. They looked around puzzled, because there was no sign of a firing squad. One of the men asked, 'Are we not then to be despatched?' They were instructed to pull their caps over their eyes and wait patiently. In a rare display of humanity, the eighteen members of the firing squad were hiding round the corner. Once the condemned men had covered their eyes, as instructed, the squad filed out silently to take up their positions. No words of command were spoken out loud, the officer giving all the necessary signals by waving a handkerchief. All three men were killed outright by the volley of shots.

The use of execution by firing squad, to act as a warning to others, is perfectly illustrated by the shooting of Admiral Byng a few years later, in 1757. That an admiral could suffer death in this way shows that this sort of death was definitely viewed as being honourable, even noble, for a member of the armed forces.

Admiral Byng commanded the British fleet at the Battle of Minorca. He drove off the French fleet, which was endeavouring to capture the island, but failed to pursue them. This decision was taken for purely military reasons, but the admiral found himself accused of cowardice in the face of the enemy and was tried before a court-martial. Byng was really a sacrifice to public opinion. People in Britain were shocked and dismayed at the loss of a British foothold in the Mediterranean, and somebody had to take responsibility. The court acquitted Admiral Byng of cowardice in the face of the enemy, but convicted him of the technical offence of 'failing to do his utmost in pursuit of the enemy'. Although this carried a mandatory death penalty, the court recommended clemency. At this point, nobody really expected the admiral to pay the ultimate price for what was, at worse, a too prudent and cautious approach in prosecuting a military action.

There was, however, to be no reprieve. On 14 March, Admiral Byng was led to the quarterdeck of the HMS *Monarch*, where he had been detained in comfortable circumstances since his trial. A squad of marines were drawn up and the admiral knelt upon a cushion. He had elected to give the signal to fire himself, by dropping a handkerchief. He died instantly.

In Europe, there was absolute astonishment at this turn of events. Voltaire satirised the affair in *Candide*, when he has somebody tell the protagonist, who witnesses the execution of an officer, '*Dans ce pays-ci, il est bon de tuer de temps en temps un amiral pour encourager les autres*' (In this country, it is thought wise to kill an admiral from time to time to encourage the others). Byng's family were outraged at the treatment which this loyal officer received from the Admiralty. The inscription on his tomb in All Saints' Church in Southill, Bedfordshire, reads:

> To the perpetual Disgrace of PUBLICK JUSTICE
> The Honble. JOHN BYNG Esqr Admiral of the Blue Fell a MARTYR to
> POLITICAL PERSECUTION March 14th in the year 1757
> When BRAVERY and LOYALTY were Insufficient Securities For the Life
> and Honour of a NAVAL OFFICER

In England, the heyday of the firing squad was, without doubt, during the First World War; hundreds of British and colonial soldiers were shot for cowardice, desertion and other breaches of military law. Precisely how many men met their deaths in this way will remain a secret until 2018, when the relevant documents will be released under the 'hundred year' rule, but the official figure of 306 is almost certainly an underestimate.

Since the late nineteenth century, there had been a tradition in Britain that military executions by firing squad were something which should only take place in foreign countries, while the army was engaged in a campaign. This was not always the case. An eighteenth-century map of London shows the execution ground at Tyburn and, nearby, a plot of land is marked as being 'Where soldiers are shot'. This unwritten law, that firing squads should not execute their own soldiers on British soil, was followed even during the frequent executions that took place during the First World War. Army deserters, apprehended in this country, were shipped back to France for court-martial and execution. As with Josef Jakobs, the only executions by firing squad to take place in Britain during the First World War, were of spies operating on behalf of Germany.

The first execution of a British soldier for desertion in the First World War took place barely a month after the outbreak of war, in August 1914. Nineteen-year-old Thomas Highgate went missing after taking part in the Battle of Mons, in the opening weeks of the war. He was arrested behind the lines, but claimed to be trying to rejoin his unit. Court-martialled for desertion on 6 September, he was shot at dawn by a firing squad just two days later. Two battalions of troops were ordered to witness his execution; one from the Dorset regiment and the other from Cheshire. News of his death was circulated widely to all units in France. It was clear that the British high command intended to take a very strong line on cowardice and desertion right from the start.

Executions became increasingly common as the war progressed; particularly after the fighting degenerated into trench warfare, as both sides became bogged down on the Western Front. It was here that the majority of executions took place during the war. It has been argued that, in fact, the British were quite sparing in their use of the firing squad to enforce military discipline. This may well be so, at least compared to the use of the death penalty by other armies involved in the conflict. And in fairness to the British generals, the vast majority of death sentences were not, in fact, carried out. Throughout the whole of the First World War, over 20,000 British and colonial soldiers were convicted of offences carrying the death penalty. Of these, only 3,000 were actually sentenced to death and ultimately only just over 300, or 10 per cent, were actually shot.

None of this alters the fact that the execution of so many young men was a pretty grim business. Many of those tried for offences such as casting away their arms or disobeying an officer, did not have access to legal advice and their trials were conducted with almost indecent haste. Some of those who faced the firing squad were also very young. Sixteen-year-old Herbert Burden, for instance, lied about his age when the war started in the summer of 1914. He pretended to be eighteen, so that he could join the Northumberland Fusiliers; fighting bravely until July of the following year. A friend from his unit had suffered a bereavement, and Private Burden left his post to comfort the young man. When his platoon was ordered to the front, Burden remained behind, and so found himself court-martialled for desertion. He was shot on 25 July, when he was still just seventeen years old; technically he was not even old enough to be in the army.

Most executions during the First World War followed a similar pattern. Any sentence of death would have to be confirmed by the commanding officer, and also by higher authorities at headquarters. Because 90 per cent of such death sentences would be commuted, the condemned man had every hope that he would not be shot. It was thought more humane to allow this belief to remain until the last possible moment. Many men were only informed of their impending execution the evening before they were to die.

The execution itself would invariably be carried out at first light. The prisoner would either be tied to a post, or seated in a chair. A piece of white lint, or paper, would be pinned over his heart and he would then be blindfolded.

The firing party, which could consist of any number of men from eight to twelve, took their places about fifteen or twenty paces from the condemned man. From then on, military routine took over and the business was conducted as briskly as if they had been on a range. The order was given and all the men would fire simultaneously at the target. Most men died instantly, although occasionally it would be necessary for the officer in charge to deliver a *coup de grâce*, by finishing the man off with a pistol shot through his head.

Almost without exception, the executions carried out by firing squad were of single men, shot one at a time. Cases of multiple executions carried out simultaneously were rare. One such occurred at four o'clock in the morning on 26 July 1915, when four men from the 3rd battalion of the Worcestershire Regiment were shot side-by-side. The British army was less sensitive about this when dealing with other races. In February 1915, an Indian regiment, the 5th (Native) Light Infantry, were stationed in Singapore. On the day of the Chinese New Year, they mutinied and in the ensuing chaos, thirty-two Europeans were killed. The mutineers were rounded up, and no fewer than 202 faced a mass court-martial. Forty-seven were sentenced to death, of whom ten were reprieved. On 23 February, twenty-one Indian soldiers were lined up against a wall and shot by a firing squad consisting of 105 British troops. This must surely rank as one of the largest firing squads ever recorded.

The last British execution by firing squad, during First World War, took place only four days before the end of hostilities. Private Louis Harris, of the 10th West Yorks, faced a court-martial on 19 October 1918. He was accused of cowardice in the face of the enemy and desertion. He was acquitted of the charge of cowardice, but convicted of desertion. At dawn on 7 November, he became the last ever British soldier to be shot for desertion. All remaining soldiers under sentence of death had their sentences commuted.

One more British soldier was to be shot by firing squad. During the Irish War of Independence, which took place shortly after the end of the First World War, there was a mutiny among an Irish regiment called the Connaught Rangers, who were stationed in India. For a while, the tricolour of Ireland flew above the military base. Of the 300-400 men who joined the mutiny, eighty-eight were arrested and faced court-martial. Some were acquitted and of those convicted, the majority received sentences of fifteen years imprisonment. Fourteen were sentenced to death. Of these, thirteen had their sentences commuted to life imprisonment. Only twenty-one-year-old Pte James Daly had his sentence confirmed. He has entered the history books as the last British soldier to be executed by a firing squad. He was shot on the morning of 2 November 1920.

Josef Jakobs may have been the only German spy to be shot by firing squad in this country during the Second World War, but eight were also executed in this way, in the same place – the Tower of London – during the First World

War. The first of these, Carl Hans Lody, was shot in November 1914. His was the first execution to take place in the Tower for over 150 years.

Carl Lody was an extraordinary man, who made a great impression on those who met him after his arrest for spying. When war broke out between Germany and Britain, in the summer of 1914, Carl Lody was a tour guide in Hamburg. He had trained as a sailor, but had been forced to give up a maritime career due to ill health. Crucially, he had at one time married an American and lived in the United States. As a result, he spoke flawless English with an American accent. As soon as England declared war on Germany, Lody volunteered to undertake espionage activities in this country. He travelled to Edinburgh, via neutral Norway, and booked into a hotel. He then visited the Firth of Forth each day and made notes on the shipping there. One of his first coded telegrams conveyed to his superiors in Germany that Royal Navy warships were due to leave port in the next day or two and as a result, a German submarine was waiting for them.

Lody became careless though and stopped encrypting his telegrams and letters. A supposed American, writing letters in German, was bound to attract attention and in October he was arrested. His trial was held in public, which was unusual for such cases. The verdict was never in doubt and on 2 November 1914, Carl Lody was sentenced to death. He had excited much admiration during his trial, for both his calm demeanour and also his steadfast patriotism in refusing to name his superior officers.

When he was led from his cell to face the firing quad on 6 November, Lody turned to the officer who was to escort him and enquired politely, 'I suppose that you will not care to shake hands with a German spy?' The officer put out his hand at once and replied, 'No, but I will shake hands with a brave man.'

In 1930, the law was changed and soldiers no longer faced the firing squad for desertion, cowardice, sleeping at their post and so on. It was, however, retained for mutiny and a few other military offences in wartime. Many senior officers campaigned for the return of the death penalty for desertion during the Second World War. In 1942, when Rommel's armour was sweeping through North Africa, the British were retreating rapidly. Sir Claude Auchinleck, Commander in Chief in the Middle East, sent a telegram to the War Office asking as a matter of urgency that the death penalty for desertion be reinstated. At the time, over 120 men were awaiting court-martial for desertion in Egypt, and a staggering 1,700 men had gone missing. So precipitate was the rout of the British forces that the Military Police were forced to open fire on their own troops, in order to halt the fleeing men.

The War Office refused Auchinleck's request, but there was one case of soldiers receiving the death penalty, even though they were not shot in the end. The so-called Salerno Mutiny occurred in October 1943. Three hundred men refused to obey orders to march, as they believed that their duty was to wait where they were, and then rejoin their own units. Almost 200 were court-martialled for mutiny. Most were sentenced to long terms of imprisonment, but the three sergeants in charge were condemned to death and faced the prospect of being shot. In the end, the sentences were commuted and all the men were freed.

There were two further executions by firing squad here, after that of Josef Jakobs. Shepton Mallet Prison, in Somerset, is the oldest prison in the United Kingdom. Parts of it date from 1610. From 1889 until 1926, it was the county prison for executions and anybody convicted of murder in Somerset faced the prospect of being hanged at Shepton Mallet. When American forces were stationed here during the Second World War, an Act of Parliament was passed which made it possible for American military justice to be carried out, including the execution of prisoners. This was the Visiting Forces Act of 1942. The Americans were allocated part of Shepton Mallet Prison and were allowed to build a new execution chamber there, which housed a gallows.

Eighteen executions were carried out at Shepton Mallet during the war. All but two of these were by hanging. For unknown reasons two men, Alex Miranda and Benjamin Pyegate, were shot by firing squad. The first to be shot was Alex Miranda. He went out drinking but was apprehended and returned to camp by the British civilian police and upon his return he shot a sleeping sergeant dead. He was sentenced to death and was executed on 30 May 1944. Benjamin Pyegate got into a fight with three fellow soldiers at his barracks in Wiltshire and stabbed one of them to death. On the morning of 28 November 1944, Pyegate was led out of his cell and tied to a post in the grounds of Shepton Mallet. A black hood was placed over his head, while a white target was fixed to his shirt over his heart. An eight-man firing squad then shot him. He was the last person ever to face a firing squad in this country.

There is some doubt as to the last time that a British firing squad carried out an execution. As has already been remarked, the use of firing squads against colonial troops always excited less disapproval than when they were used to execute British men. In July 1941, an army driver called Shabani bin Salu was shot for murder in Africa. The following year, a number of Sri Lankan soldiers were sentenced to death and executed for mutiny, the only soldiers in the Second World War to be executed for such an offence. They were, however, hanged rather than shot. It seems likely that Josef Jakobs was the last person to be executed anywhere in the world by a British firing squad.

The death penalty under military law for mutiny remained after the end of the Second World War; it was a theoretical possibility in the armed forces until 1998, when Britain finally and formally abandoned all capital punishment.

BURNING AT THE STAKE

There can be few ways of meeting one's death worse than being burnt alive. For several centuries, being burnt alive was the prescribed penalty in Britain for a number of offences. This method of execution was used against both men and women. However, in later years, it was almost exclusively used for the execution of women. To begin with, it is necessary to clear up one misunderstanding about this form of execution. Burning at the stake was never used for the execution of witches in England. It was imposed in Scotland for witchcraft, but in England, convicted witches and sorcerers were hanged. The mistaken idea that English witches were burnt has been fostered by films such as the Hammer Horror film *Witchfinder General*, which was popular during the 1960s.

The first instances of execution by being burnt alive in Britain, are recorded by Julius Caesar in the *Gallic War*. He claimed that the Celts built huge wicker-work figures, filled them with condemned criminals and then set fire to them. The Bible prescribes death by burning for certain crimes, such as sexual immorality. Also in the Bible, we learn that sinners will burn for all eternity. This probably fostered the belief that heretics should be given a taste of this punishment (which they would experience in the next world) right here on earth. In 1184, the Catholic Church declared, at the Synod of Verona, that death by burning should be officially adopted as the penalty for heresy. At a time when most people in Europe looked forward to a physical resurrection, this was an especially terrible fate. It more or less ruled out the person from

rising from the grave on the last day. This was a time when those who had had
a limb amputated took great care to preserve it so that it might be buried with
them, ready for Judgement Day.

The first person that we know to have been burned at the stake for heresy
was a deacon from Oxford, who was executed in this way in 1222. His crime
was to have fallen in love with Jewess; he then converted to Judaism so that he
could marry her. In 1401, during the reign of Henry IV, the Statute of Heresy
was passed in England, which gave clergy the authority to arrest and question those suspected of heresy. It was this Act, *De Heretico Comburendo*, which
marked the beginning of regular judicial burnings in this country. One of the
first to be convicted under this Act was a priest called William Sawtrey. He
become disillusioned with the Catholic Church and so joined the Lollards. In
February 1401, he was brought before Archbishop Thomas Arundel and tried
for heresy. He was found guilty and burned the following month.

In 1414, another Heresy Act was passed, which made the offence of heresy
a civil, as well as an ecclesiastical, offence. It was a violation of this Act which
brought about one of the rare cases of the burning of a supposed witch in
England. Margaret Jordemaine was accused of trying to kill King Henry VI
by the use of witchcraft. She was convicted and burned alive on 27 October
1441. It is a debateable point as to whether this woman was burnt for witchcraft, heresy or the attempted murder of the sovereign. The Old Testament
places an absolute prohibition on any sort of sorcery or witchcraft, and more-
over recommends the death penalty for witches. Exodus 22:18 says, 'Thou
shalt not suffer a witch to live'. Fortune-telling and other acts of magic were
therefore ecclesiastical crimes.

For the century or so following the passing of the two Heresy Acts, executions for this crime continued at a slow but steady pace. In 1533, Henry VIII
repealed the 1401 Act, which ensured that anybody accused of heresy would
have to be indicted through the normal courts. This removed some of the
power which the clergy had enjoyed in the matter of heresy cases. It was part
of Henry's attempt to remove power from the Church and transfer it to the
state; the same process which led to the Dissolution of the Monasteries and
the establishment of the Anglican Church. During Henry's reign, from 1509
to 1547, just over eighty people were burnt for heresy in England.

In London, burnings at the stake almost invariably took place at Smithfield,
the site of the meat market today. An example of the sort of person being
burned at that time is given by Ann Askew, otherwise known as the 'Fair
Gospeller'. Ann was a young woman from Lincolnshire, who had very strong
views about religion. She believed that the Catholic Church was quite
wrong about many things, and because of Henry VIII's break with Rome,
she thought it safe to voice her heterodox beliefs openly. She left her husband
and came to London, where she preached and wrote about her views on

the Gospels. Unfortunately, she became involved with some Protestants who were suspected of plotting with the King's wife, Katherine Parr. Ann Askew did not realise her danger, and seemed surprised to be arrested and charged with heresy. By the day of her execution, she had been tortured so severely that she could not walk; she had to be carried to the stake at Smithfield in a chair. Even when she was fixed to the stake, she was offered a pardon if she should recant. She rebuked the man offering her this option, saying, 'I came not hither to deny my Lord and Master!' It is said that she did not scream until the flames reached her chest.

What was the actual cause of death when somebody was burned alive in this way? There were three possible ways of dying. The most fortunate ones swiftly lost consciousness, after inhaling the carbon monoxide produced by the burning faggots. This would have been a relatively merciful death indeed. Others breathed in the hot air, which caused their lungs to swell, causing them to choke to death. If not as painless as being asphyxiated by carbon monoxide, this too was a relatively quick and painless death. However, not everybody was lucky enough to die in these ways. For a description of the full horrors of being burnt at the stake, we must turn to the example of somebody burned when Bloody Mary was Queen. A fanatical Catholic, Mary was merciless when it came to persecuting Protestants. Almost 300 people were burnt for heresy in the course of her brief reign.

John Hooper was appointed Bishop of Gloucester when Edward VI became King on the death of his father, Henry VIII. Hooper had spent a good deal of time in Europe, and was a devout Protestant. When Mary succeeded her brother, Hooper was replaced as Bishop of Gloucester and sent to prison. He was tried for heresy, and became the first former bishop to be burnt under Mary's rule. Although he was tried in London, it was decided to send him back to Gloucester to be executed. He met his death on the morning of 8 February 1555; the event being witnessed by a crowd estimated at over 7,000. It was a cold morning, and the kindling provided for the fire consisted of bundles of moist green rushes. When he prayed before the execution, a pardon from the Queen was laid before him – he rejected it courteously. A contemporary account describes the horrific manner of his death:

> Command was now given that the fire should be kindled. But because there were not more green fagots than two horses could carry, it kindled not speedily, and was a pretty while also before it took the reeds upon the fagots. At length it burned about him, but the wind having full strength at that place, and being a lowering cold morning, it blew the flame from him, so that he was in a manner little more than touched by the fire. Within a space after, a few dry fagots were brought, and a new fire kindled with fagots, (for there were no more reeds) and those burned at the nether parts, but

had small power above, because of the wind, saving that it burnt his hair and scorched his skin a little. In the time of which fire, even as at the first flame, he prayed, saying mildly, and not very loud, but as one without pain, 'O Jesus, Son of David, have mercy upon me, and receive my soul!' After the second fire was spent, he wiped both his eyes with his hands, and beholding the people, he said with an indifferent, loud voice, 'For God's love, good people, let me have more fire!' and all this while his nether parts did burn; but the fagots were so few that the flame only singed his upper parts. The third fire was kindled within a while after, which was more extreme than the other two. In this fire he prayed with a loud voice, 'Lord Jesus, have mercy upon me! Lord Jesus receive my spirit!' And these were the last words he was heard to utter. But when he was black in the mouth, and his tongue so swollen that he could not speak, yet his lips went until they were shrunk to the gums: and he knocked his breast with his hands until one of his arms fell off, and then knocked still with the other, while the fat, water, and blood dropped out at his fingers' ends, until by renewing the fire, his strength was gone, and his hand clave fast in knocking to the iron upon his breast. Then immediately bowing forwards, he yielded up his spirit. Thus was he three quarters of an hour or more in the fire. Even as a lamb, patiently he abode the extremity thereof, neither moving forwards, backwards, nor to any side; but he died as quietly as a child in his bed.

This was the reality of burning at the stake; the most hideous death that can be imagined.

It was during the reign of Queen Mary (Bloody Mary as she became known), that executions for heresy began to be a regular feature of the English scene. In some European countries, most notably Spain, there were huge carnivals which culminated in the mass burning of heretics who had been condemned by the Inquisition. The *Auto de Fe*, as these events were known, never really took off in this country. Following the reign of Henry VIII, and the Reformation, enthusiasm for the Catholic Church among many ordinary people was lukewarm, and nobody apart from Mary and her bishops seemed to have much of an appetite for the burnings, which had been so frequent during the five years that Mary was Queen.

Mary's marriage to Prince Philip of Spain, in the second year of her reign, probably led to the so-called Marian Persecutions of Protestants. Mary's fanaticism, coupled with the legacy of the religious intolerance of the Spanish Inquisition, seemed to set the stage for the mass burnings of those who refused to acknowledge the supremacy of the Catholic Church. No wonder there was great uneasiness about the Queen marrying Philip of Spain. Many people feared that the next step would be the arrival of the Inquisition themselves, to enforce orthodoxy upon the people of England. In fact, Philip and his advisers regarded the mass burnings which began in England as being counter-productive to the return of England to the Catholic fold. Gruesome executions of this sort had the effect of making the English less and less enamoured of the Catholic Church. During Henry's reign, one or two people a year were burned for heresy. While Mary was Queen, this rate increased twenty-five fold.

The first victim of Mary's hard line on heresy was John Rogers, who had been the vicar of St Sepulchre Church in London. He had converted to Protestantism as a young man and when Mary reintroduced the Heresy Acts, which her father had scrapped, it was only a matter of time before the first high-profile protestant priest was brought to trial. Rogers was that most detestable object to orthodox Catholics, a priest with a wife and children. Following his condemnation, he asked permission for his family to visit him; it was refused. According to one witness, he died peacefully, washing his hands in the flames. The horrors which took place at Smithfield have left no permanent mark upon the place, other than the fact that when the present gardens were being laid out there, a layer of ash was discovered a few feet below the surface.

The burnings in Mary's reign sometimes resembled the *Auto de Fe* of the Spanish Inquisition. This was because, in addition to individual executions, there were also mass burnings. Today, the district of Stratford lies in the heart of East London. In the sixteenth century though, it was a small village in Essex. There was a large village green, which has shrunk greatly; all that is left is the church of St John and its graveyard. Urban development has left this patch of green stranded as a traffic island. Anybody taking the trouble to look round the churchyard will find an impressive monument, erected in the nineteenth century. It commemorates the greatest mass burning of men and women in British judicial history, which took place upon that very spot. On 27 June 1556, eleven men and two women, from all over the county, were brought to Stratford Green, where stakes had been set up. All the victims were offered free pardons if they would only abjure their heresy and attend the Catholic mass. They were obstinate Protestants and all refused to do so. The eleven men were chained to the stakes but the women, one of whom was pregnant, were left unbound and free to walk around in the flames. Some of those executed that day were guilty of nothing more than declining to attend mass and in some cases reading the Bible in English. Today, a monument over 50ft high marks the spot where this, the greatest mass burning in British history, took place.

An incredible feature of the executions by burning, during Mary's reign, was the completely voluntary nature of the deaths. These were willing martyrs, who embraced death of their own free will. This element of choice is of course wholly lacking in most executions. Pardons from the Queen were lying ready to be handed to many of the important victims of burning, such as bishops and other high-ranking churchmen. Even for the ordinary person, all that was necessary to avoid this hideous death was for those condemned to admit that they were wrong and agree to attend mass in a Catholic church. This made those who suffered death in this way either incredibly noble and principled or exceedingly foolish and strong-headed, according to one's point of view.

Burning for heresy more or less ended when Mary was succeeded by her sister, Elizabeth. There were one or two odd cases, but the practice ended completely in 1612. In that year, Edward Wightman, a Baptist, was burned at the stake for heresy in Staffordshire. All those who were subsequently burned were women, and there is a very curious reason for this. The penalty prescribed for treason was hanging, drawing and quartering, but it was felt that this would be an indecent spectacle if inflicted upon a woman. Women convicted of treason were therefore sentenced to be burned. Ann Boleyn and Catherine Howard, the supposedly adulterous wives of Henry VIII, were tried for treason and both were sentenced to be burned alive. Henry, however, commuted the sentence to beheading. Lady Jane Grey, the nine-day Queen, who was executed at the age of seventeen, was also sentenced to be burned alive, but Mary commuted this to beheading. Others were not so fortunate.

The Treason Act of 1351 specified various kinds of treason, apart from the obvious one of betraying or waging war against the Monarch. Among these were a wife murdering her husband, a servant killing their master and a prelate harming his bishop. These were all thought to be forms of rebellion against the natural order of things, as bad as treason but on a smaller scale; hence the expression *petit* or petty treason. This meant that a woman who killed her husband was guilty of treason and could be burned alive, as could a maid who killed her master or mistress. With the end of burning for heresy, this effectively meant that the only people who would be burned alive in Britain would be women.

There was one other form of treason which affected women, and brought them into hazard of being burned at the stake. This was forging currency. Forgery was viewed as touching upon the very stability of the country, almost waging war upon it. This offence was also treated as treason.

As the seventeenth century drew on, it became common for women who were to be burned to be strangled first. This was certainly a more merciful death than that of being burnt alive. Even so, the last instance of a woman being deliberately burned alive, without being strangled first, took place fairly late in that century.

In the aftermath of the Duke of Monmouth's rebellion against his uncle, James II, there was a witch-hunt for anybody who had assisted or offered any comfort to men from Monmouth's army. King James had declared publicly

The execution of Sir Walter Raleigh; the high block in operation.

The site of the Tyburn gallows.

The execution by hanging, drawing and quartering of Guy Fawkes and his fellow conspirators.

The Banqueting Hall; site of Charles I's execution today.

The Edinburgh Maiden in the National Museum of Scotland. (Wikimedia, Kim Tragnor)

Crowds at the execution of Lord Balmerino and the Earl of Kilmarnock on Tower Hill.

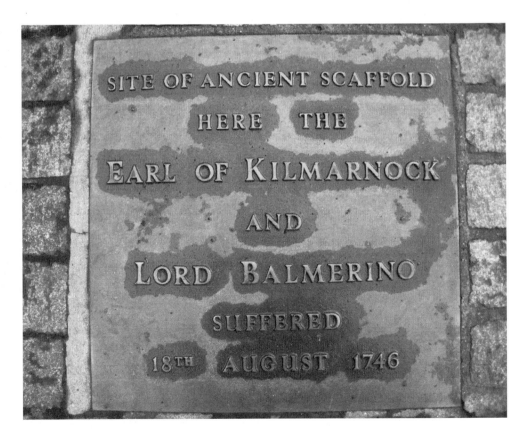

SITE OF ANCIENT SCAFFOLD
HERE THE
EARL OF KILMARNOCK
AND
LORD BALMERINO
SUFFERED
18TH AUGUST 1746

A plaque on Tower Hill, where beheadings took place until the eighteenth century.

Temple Bar gateway; where decapitated heads were displayed until the late eighteenth century.

A typical execution by block and axe.

Beheading with a sword; not a common method in this country.

An early example of hanging, drawing and quartering; the execution of Hugh
Despenser in 1326.

The burning of a priest.

A group of men and women burned together during the Marian persecutions.

A hanging in the nineteenth century; the hangman is William Marwood, the man who devised the so-called 'long drop'.

The Shot at Dawn memorial at the National Memorial Arboretum. (Wikimedia, NMA Guide).

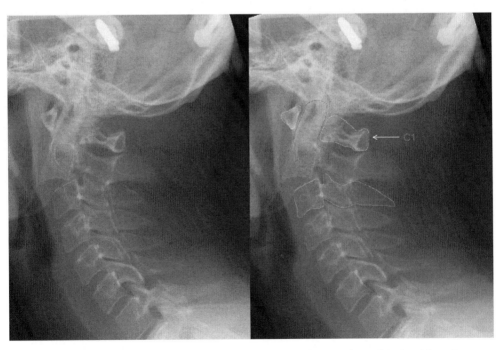

The classic 'hangman's fracture of the neck'; an ideal not always achieved in legal hanging. (Wikimedia, Lucien Moufils)

Possible forerunner to the Halifax Gibbet; a beheading machine supposedly operating in Ireland in 1307.

Smithfield today.

The monument to the
martyrs of Stratford.

The Halifax Gibbet. Although this machine is a replica, it stands upon the original platform and steps. (Wikimedia, scarletharlot69)

The execution of Charles I outside the banqueting hall in Whitehall.

Typical execution at Tyburn. The triangular gallows may be seen in the background. This engraving is by Hogarth.

The execution of seventeen-year-old Lady Jane Grey in 1554; an infamous British beheading.

The gory business of hanging, drawing and quartering.

that of all forms of treason, he regarded the hiding of traitors from his vengeance as the worst imaginable. When a middle-aged woman called Elizabeth Gaunt allowed a man called Burton to stay at her home, she was doing precisely this, as she probably knew that he was a supporter of Monmouth fleeing from justice. In an act of appalling injustice, Burton himself was allowed to turn King's Evidence and was pardoned in exchange for speaking as a witness against the woman who had sheltered him. He walked free after Elizabeth Gaunt's trial.

The trial took place at the Old Bailey on 19 October 1685 and it was pretty much an open and shut case. There was no doubt that Burton had been hidden in Elizabeth Gaunt's house, nor that she was ignorant of his background. Indeed, it was suggested during the trial that she was operating a 'safe house' for rebels and smuggling them out of the country to refuge in the Netherlands. She was convicted and the sentence was read to her:

> That you are to be carried back to the place from whence you came, from thence you are to be drawn upon a hurdle to the place of execution, and there you are to be burned to death; and the Lord have smercy upon your soul.

It was generally assumed that this was merely a formality, and that she would either be pardoned or, at worst, the sentence would be commuted to beheading; in fact, neither happened. Not only did King James not commute the sentence, but he also made it clear that he expected the sentence to be adhered to; Elizabeth Gaunt was to be burned to death rather than being strangled first.

Four days after her trial, Elizabeth Gaunt was drawn to Tyburn on a hurdle and made ready for her ordeal. A stout post had been hammered into the ground and she was chained to this, the chains being secured by a blacksmith and nailed into place. Sheaves of reeds and bundles of dry wood were arranged around her and the fire was set. She seems to have died fairly quickly, but there was a general feeling of anger towards James II, for insisting on this barbaric ritual. This was the last time that any woman was executed in this country for a political offence.

In Scotland, the occasional witch was still being burned – the last execution for witchcraft being in 1727 – but in the rest of the country the only women being burned had either murdered their husbands or had been caught committing forgery. Burning at the stake was an infrequent occurrence during the eighteenth century; in the first thirty years of that century, only ten women were burnt. Eight of these were sentenced for High Treason – which meant coining – and two for killing their husbands. Nine of these women were strangled before their bodies were reduced to ashes, but one suffered the full horror of being burned alive. This was an accident, but that can hardly have been any consolation.

Catherine Hayes was a thirty-five-year-old married woman living in London. Her husband was quite well off, but Catherine had a voracious sexual appetite which he was unable to satisfy. He also failed to provide her with as much money as she thought she needed. She persuaded her husband to invite a lodger to stay at their house. Unknown to him, this eighteen-year-old boy, Thomas Billings, was actually her illegitimate son. No sooner had he moved in than Catherine began an incestuous affair with him. Another lodger moved in, and she also began sleeping with him. At some stage, she persuaded her son to kill her husband, which he did with an axe. The other lodger, Thomas Wood, helped with the murder and the two men rounded the thing off by decapitating their victim, in an effort to prevent the corpse from being identified. They threw the head into the Thames and dismembered the rest of the body, scattering it about London.

The head was found floating in the river and placed on public display in a churchyard, where it was recognised. Catherine Hayes and her two lovers found themselves in the dock at the Old Bailey, where the two men were found guilty of murder and Catherine was convicted of *petit* treason. Wood died in prison, but Catherine Hayes and her son were taken with a batch of other condemned men to Tyburn. On 9 May 1726, she had to witness her son being hanged before she herself was dealt with.

Richard Arnet, the executioner, secured Catherine to a wooden post and piled two cartloads of brushwood round her. He then arranged a cord round her neck and passed it through a hole in the post. Having made these preliminary arrangements, Arnet set fire to the brushwood, then nipped round the back of the stake to pull on the rope and strangle the woman, before the flames took hold. At that point, disaster struck. The wind suddenly changed and blew the flames into Richard Arnet's face. He jumped back, letting go of the cord, which then fell into the fire, which by now was taking hold vigorously. Catherine Hayes was screaming loudly and was seen by spectators to be pushing away the burning wood surrounding her. At this point the executioner, feeling that he had botched the thing, tried to make amends by putting the wretched woman out of her misery. He took a large piece of timber and pitched it at her head, intending perhaps to knock her out. It proved to be a case of overkill because, in the words of a witness, the chunk of wood 'broke her skull, when her brains came plentifully out.'

The burning of women was not, of course, limited to London. As the eighteenth century progressed, and the Industrial Revolution was in full swing, such executions took place across the length and breadth of Britain: at Chelmsford and Northampton in 1735, Winchester and Guildford in 1738, Gloucester and Wells in 1753; the burnings mainly for coining continued.

However, it was becoming increasingly plain that this dreadful spectacle had no place in an enlightened society. But with the law as it was, the judge had no option but to pass this sentence for the prescribed felonies.

It was events in the capital which finally forced the authorities to confront what was becoming a grotesque anachronism. In 1783, executions at Tyburn stopped. From that year, the hangings which had taken place at Tyburn took place outside Newgate Prison, in the heart of London. Hangings were popular enough, but it was to be another three years before the full implications of the decision to move the site – from Tyburn to the vicinity of St Paul's Cathedral – really struck home for Londoners.

Shortly before Christmas 1785, a woman rented a room in Drury Lane under the name Mrs Brown. She had been recommended to the landlord by Francis Hardy. The woman's real name was Phoebe Harris and her occupation was coining. She carried this out by means of what was called 'clipping'. If we look at a modern pound coin, we will see that it has a milled edge. These days, this is done purely for decoration, but the custom of giving milled edges to silver and gold coins had a very practical motive. 'Clippers' would shave the edges of coins, and when they had enough silver or gold shavings, they would melt the metal down and use it to cast new coins. This was the business in which Phoebe Harris was engaged and it was a capital crime.

Later, there were rumours that Francis Hardy was having an affair with Phoebe Harris, an allegation which he vehemently denied. What is not in dispute is that on the morning of 11 February 1786s Hardy laid information that Phoebe Harris was a forger of currency. She was arrested later that day; a few hours later, Francis Hardy took her teenage daughter to live with him, ostensibly as a servant. It is hard to avoid the suspicion that there was more to Hardy's denunciation than mere public spiritedness.

When the police raided the room in Drury Lane, they found another woman on the premises as well as Phoebe Harris. She too was arrested, as was her brother when he arrived at the room later that day. There was ample evidence in the form of moulds, ladles and newly made coins. Phoebe Harris, Elizabeth Yelland and her brother were all charged:

> That they, on the 11th of February last, one piece of false, feigned, and counterfeit money and coin, to the likeness and similitude of the good, legal, and silver coin of this realm, called a shilling, falsely, deceitfully, feloniously, and traitorously did counterfeit and coin, against the duty of their allegiance, and against the statute.

At their trial, Phoebe Harris alone was convicted and sentenced to be burnt at the stake.

At eight o'clock in the morning of Wednesday, 21 June 1786, the six men who had been sentenced to death in the same sessions as Phoebe Harris were led out of Newgate Prison and hanged on the 'new drop' gallows. There was an unusually large crowd that day, presumably because the burning of a woman in the heart of the city was something of a novelty. A 10ft-high stake had been erected in Newgate Street and a little after eight o'clock, Phoebe Harris was led from the debtor's door of the prison to the place of her execution. According to witnesses, she was utterly terrified, shaking so much that she could hardly walk. An iron bracket had been fixed to the top of the stake, from which a noose was hanging. The condemned woman was made to stand on a stool while the noose was placed round her neck. After a short prayer, the stool was knocked away and she choked to death. She apparently took several minutes to die, gasping and coughing noisily. Once she was dead, the executioner fixed her body securely to the stake and the fire was lit. It took hours for her body to be completely consumed by the flames and a number of local people were made ill by the smell.

Before the execution, local residents and merchants had protested at the idea of burning a woman in the very centre of the financial district. *The Times* added its voice to the controversy, saying in an editorial:

> The execution of a woman for coining on Wednesday morning, reflects a scandal upon the law and was not only inhuman, but shamefully indelicate and shocking. Why should the law in this species of offence inflict a severer punishment upon a woman, than a man?

There were only to be two more executions of this sort. On 28 June 1788, Margaret Sullivan was hanged and burned; and on 17 March 1789, Catherine Murphy suffered the same fate. By this time, moves were already afoot to put a stop to this barbarous practice.

In the spring of 1790, an MP called Benjamin Hammett rose to speak in the Commons. He told the House that he had been the Sheriff of London at the time of Catherine Murphy's burning and that, as such, it had been his job to supervise the process. He explained to the House that technically, the law required that women be burned alive and that, as Sheriff, he could have been prosecuted for allowing Murphy to be hanged before being burned. The 1790 Treason Act was passed a short time later, this made hanging the punishment for both men and women found guilty of forging currency. There were to be no more burnings at the stake.

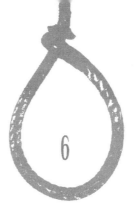

THE BLOODY CODE:
THE HEYDAY OF BRITISH HANGING

During the eighteenth century, a gradual change took place in Britain, as the country moved from an agrarian to an industrial society. The most obvious feature of this sociological phenomenon was the movement of large numbers of former agricultural workers to the cities, swelling their populations enormously. Such a large-scale transfer of populations inevitably led to problems, as people found difficulty in adjusting to the new urban society that was being created. It also created turmoil in the countryside as the depopulation of rural areas caused a radical reappraisal about the way that society worked, or ought to work. The population of London was already growing rapidly in the late seventeenth century; it doubled between 1650 and 1700. This increase, in the size of towns and cities, accelerated from 1700 onwards. In the last thirty years of the eighteenth century, for example, the number of people living in Manchester increased four-fold.

Many of those moving to the cities were very poor, which inevitably led a good number of them turning to crime to survive. They picked pockets, stole from shops, forged coins, broke into houses, robbed passers-by and came up with innumerable other ways of getting their hands on other people's money and property. The response of those in charge was to combat this crimewave by instilling fear into people, with an increased number of executions. At the restoration of the monarchy in 1660, there were around fifty capital crimes; less that a century later, in 1750, this had risen to a 160. By 1815, a person in Britain could be hanged for any of 220 offences, many of them unbelievably trivial by today's standards.

This huge expansion of capital crimes became known as the Bloody Code, and for over a century it was believed to be the best means of keeping crime under control in this country. What sort of offences merited hanging during the rule of the Bloody Code? Damaging Westminster Bridge was one. Incredible as it may seem, vandalism to this bridge could theoretically result in being hanged. A particularly savage law introduced at this time, and one which is frequently cited as the epitome of the Bloody Code, was the Black Act of 1722; it is often known as the 'Waltham' Black Act, in reference to the forest of Waltham in Hampshire. Its official title, nowhere near as catchy as 'The Black Act', was:

> An Act for the more effectual punishing of wicked and evil disposed Persons going armed in Disguise, and doing Injuries and Violences to the Persons and Properties of His Majesty's Subjects, and for the more speedy bringing the Offenders to Justice.

Landowners in the south of England had been troubled by an increase in poaching and vandalism on their estates. The Black Act aimed to put a stop to this, by hanging anybody who looked as though he might even be preparing to poach deer. After the passage of this notorious Act, it was a hanging matter to chase deer in a forest or estate. It was also a capital crime to black one's face or to wear a disguise in a forest. Other hanging offences, which already existed, were as varied as associating with Gypsies, sending threatening letters, felling someone else's trees, stealing a horse, engaging in acts of male homosexuality, stealing from a rabbit warren, shoplifting and impersonating a Chelsea Pensioner.

Even at the time, many people in Britain were disturbed at the introduction of such a far-reaching piece of legislation, which created so many capital crimes. Gilbert White, better known as the author of *The Natural History of Selborne*, was disgusted by the Black Act, describing it as 'severe and sanguinary'. He wrote that, 'it comprehends more felonies than any law that ever was framed before.'

It might have been thought that these ferocious laws would have had the effect of reducing the crime rate, but this is not what happened at all. There were several reasons. First, it was very unlikely that one would be caught for any sort of crime in the eighteenth century, when the Bloody Code held sway. There were no police forces to speak of and no detectives at all. If one was not actually caught red-handed committing a crime, there was every reason to believe that they would escape any repercussions. Even the fiercest punishment in the world will not deter a potential criminal, if the chances of being apprehended are negligible. Another reason for the lack of efficacy in the discouraging of crime by the regular hangings was that people had become hardened to the sight of death. Public executions were meant to be solemn and awe-inspiring occasions, but they degenerated into something akin to carnivals. The regular, first Monday of the month hanging days at the Tyburn gallows were popularly known as 'The Tyburn Fair'. There were eight such hanging days each year, and the very fact that they were known as 'fairs' suggests that there was nothing solemn or awe-inspiring about them.

Hanging days at Tyburn were seen by most as a kind of bank holiday entertainment. Apprentices were traditionally given the day off, and in an age without television, internet or computer games, these events were greatly looked forward to as a break in the monotony of everyday life. There was a long and lively procession from Newgate Prison to the site of the gallows, and although, as the crow flies, the distance is only three miles or so, it generally took hours for the cart to travel those few short miles. Some of those condemned were slumped half dead with terror by their coffin, which travelled with them, but others were in good spirits and engaged in lively banter with those thronging the roads. It was quite something to be able to say that you had exchanged words with this or that famous highwayman; the equivalent today perhaps of having met a well-known celebrity.

At Tyburn itself stands were set up which, for a price, would guarantee a good view of the hanging. Nearby houses rented out rooms for the day if they happened to have a window overlooking the gallows. Soft drinks were sold, snacks of all sorts were available, souvenir printed confessions hawked around – many of them spurious; it was probably very much like a present day carnival or rock concert. The site of the gallows is marked today by a plaque on the traffic island at the Marble Arch end of Edgeware Road.

And of course, the pickpockets had a profitable time of it. Although picking pockets was itself a hanging offence under the provisions of the Bloody Code, this did not deter thieves when they found themselves in crowded places such as this. The chances of detection being virtually zero and the potential gains enormous, it was inevitable that many would take the risk of stealing. A priest, who spoke with a great number of condemned men and women at the height of Tyburn's activities, learned that over 90 per cent of those under sentence of death had witnessed hangings themselves. These had not had the least effect upon their subsequent behaviour. When death becomes a form of entertainment in this way, people are quickly inured to the sight and no longer regard it as being such a terrible thing.

There was yet another reason why the Bloody Code did not work; rather than increasing respect for the law, it actually brought it into disrepute. This was brought about by the practice of what became known as 'Pious Perjury'. Because the law was so harsh on relatively trifling offences, juries became reluctant to convict if this would mean a sentence of death. This was especially the case with women and young people. At the 1715 Sessions in central

London, for example, half the women on trial for their lives were acquitted. Of those who were found guilty, half escaped the death sentence by the exercise of the jury of 'Pious Perjury'. If, for instance, the accused had been taken in the act of shoplifting goods worth £2, then this would entail a mandatory death penalty; stealing goods over the value of 5s from a shop being a hanging offence. The jury would often acquit altogether if the prisoner seemed poor or young and when they did bring in a guilty verdict, they would specifically reduce the value of the goods stolen. In the case of the hypothetical person above, who had stolen £2 worth of goods from a shop, the jury might convict her of stealing only 4s 10d worth.

While quite understandable, this sort of well-intentioned dishonesty on the part of juries made a mockery of the law. The overall effect was that not only criminals, but also law-abiding men serving on juries, began to view the law of England with contempt and cooperate in frustrating it. This is not a healthy state of affairs. A real life example will illustrate how things worked.

In 1701, a child called Nathaniel Hawes was born in Norfolk. His father died a year after he was born and the child was sent to live with relatives in Hertfordshire. As a teenager he was apprenticed to an upholsterer in London. He soon fell in with bad company and was dismissed for stealing from his employer. His next boss found so much going missing, that he had young Nathaniel prosecuted. In particular, he had lost £8 worth of cloth, a very serious financial blow. At the age of twenty, Nathaniel Hawes found himself in the dock at the Old Bailey, facing a capital charge. He was fortunate in his jury. Theft of goods from an employer, valued at over £2, carried the death penalty, but in this case the jury decided that the cloth had only been worth 39s, that is to say 1s short of £2. In a later chapter, we shall see what ultimately became of Nathaniel Hawes.

To get a flavour of how the death penalty operated during the eighteenth century, it might be instructive to follow the procession from Newgate Prison to Tyburn, and see how the whole thing would have appeared to those taking part.

We begin on the day before the executions. This was a Sunday and so the condemned men would attend chapel. That night, the last of their lives, a gruesome and disturbing ritual ensured that they did not forget the ordeal facing them the next day. Robert Dowes, a pious man in the late sixteenth century, was greatly worried about the state of the souls of those lying under sentence of death at Newgate. In his will, he left a bequest which made provision for reminding these unfortunate people of what awaited them. At midnight the bell in the tower of nearby St Sepulchre's Church tolled and a man rang a hand-bell in the precincts of the prison, within earshot of the condemned cells. After he had attracted their attention he then recited the following piece of doggerel:

All you that in the condemned hole do lie,
Prepare you, for tomorrow you shall die,
Watch all and pray: the hour is drawing near,
That you before the Almighty must appear.
Examine well yourselves, in time repent,
That you may not to eternal flames be sent,
And when St Sepulchre's bell in the morning tolls,
The Lord above have mercy on your souls.

In the morning, the condemned prisoners were taken to the press room to have their chains struck off. Their arms were then tied to their bodies at the elbow, leaving their hands free. They then mounted into horse-drawn carts for the journey to Tyburn. Often, their coffins went with them in the same cart. As a final macabre touch, nooses were placed round their necks.

The bell of St Sepulchre's tolled dolorously while the procession formed; the front carts containing those convicted of the most serious offences. Some of the condemned dressed in their finest clothes, eager to make a good impression on their last day of life. Earl Ferrers, who died upon the experimental new gallows erected at Tyburn in 1759, wore his wedding suit. This was white satin embroidered with silver thread and Ferrers remarked that, 'this is at least as good an occasion for putting them on as that for which they were first made.' He also rode to his death in a grand mourning coach, rather than the more usual horse and cart. Others were more pragmatic about the question of clothing. Since the clothes of an executed person were traditionally seen as a perk of the hangman, some went to their hanging wearing nothing more elaborate than a shirt or nightgown, reasoning that it did not make sense to gift their clothes to the executioner. Sometimes, this desire to cheat the hangman of what he saw as his rightful property provided the crowd with some extra amusement.

Hannah Dagoe was due to be hanged at Tyburn. She was a tough Irish woman, who had been condemned for burglary, then, as now, an unusual offence for a woman. She was determined that the executioner should not have her clothes and so when the cart in which she was travelling reached the gallows, she began stripping off her clothing and throwing it to the crowd. The hangman argued with her about this and a fight ensued, in which he was nearly pushed out of the cart. The spectators roared their approval at Hannah's resistance. There was a further struggle before it was possible to get the rope around her neck and no sooner had this been done, than the angry woman leaped from the cart, breaking her neck at once.

Before the procession left the vicinity of St Sepulchre's Church, another part of the ritual paid for by Robert Dowe's legacy was enacted. The man who had rung his hand-bell in the prison on the previous night appeared again and rang his bell once more, to attract attention and demand silence. Then, with the bell of St Sepulchre's striking in the background, he read out the following speech:

> All good people, pray heartily unto God for these poor sinners who are going to their death, for whom this great bell doth toll. You that are condemned to die, repent with lamentable tears: ask mercy of the Lord for the salvation of your souls through the merits, death and passion of Jesus Christ, who now sits at the right hand of God, to make intercession for as many of you as penitently return unto him. Lord have mercy upon you. Christ have mercy upon you.

The carts, accompanied by an escort of soldiers, now set off for Tyburn. Although only the distance between St Paul's and Marble Arch stations on the Central Line tube, this journey typically took between two and three hours. The reason for this is that there were a number of stops en route, at various pubs and alehouses. One of these was at St Giles, roughly where Tottenham Court tube station is today. Inns were only too happy to offer free drinks for condemned men and women on their way to execution. As the carts stopped and the drinks were dispensed, many in the following crowd would also take the opportunity to eat and drink. It was good business to have this vast throng of people halted outside one's establishment.

Queen Matilda, wife of Henry I, had instituted the custom of condemned men and woman being given a drink at St Giles while en route to execution. A hospital originally stood here and the drinks would be handed out there. This stopped in 1750, but a nearby alehouse was swift to take over and offer the service to the condemned. The Bowel Inn made a roaring trade from those in the crowd who *were* paying for their drinks. Other public houses got in on the act and it was not uncommon for those about to be hanged to be half drunk by the time they arrived at the gallows.

We have been looking at the procession from Tyburn, but this sort of scene would be replicated at hangings in most towns. The prisons themselves were generally in the centre of town and the hangings, as we have seen, took place on the outskirts. This inevitably meant a journey of some kind from prison to gallows and human nature being what it is, these events turned into an enjoyable distraction from the routine of everyday life.

Prisoners on their way to be hanged behaved in differing ways. Some, such as the highwaymen, behaved like rock stars on their way to a concert; flirting outrageously with young women whom they spotted among the spectators, bantering with others and generally conducting themselves with grace and charm. This always went down well with the crowd. Others though were prostrate with fear. A number fainted and lay unconscious in the bottom of the cart. These excited only the scorn of those watching. And then there were those felons whose crimes were of such a nature as to cause them to forfeit all sympathy. Elizabeth Brownrigg, who was hanged in 1767, was one such individual. She had cruelly mistreated a succession of young girls whom she had acquired as servants from workhouses. She tried to cut out the tongue of one and whipped them all so brutally that one of the girls died. She was pelted with all sorts of filth on her way to Tyburn and the verbal abuse and rain of missiles did not even stop at the gallows, when she was trying to pray.

The overall mood of those following the condemned to the gallows was probably similar to those attending a carnival today. Like any disorganised mob, they could turn ugly or be provoked to laughter – depending upon the circumstance. Their only motive for being there in the first place was to be entertained and amused. Many sensitive writers who witnessed the behaviour of the crowds who gathered to watch public hangings, were appalled at the levity displayed and the callousness which was shown towards fellow creatures about to die a painful and humiliating death.

Some years after hangings had stopped at Tyburn, Charles Dickens wrote a description of the crowd at a public execution which has never been rivalled. Although he is talking about a hanging which took place in 1849, the behaviour of those watching was no different from the Tyburn mob. On 13 November 1849, this letter by Dickens appeared in *The Times*:

I was a witness of the execution at Horsemonger Lane this morning. I went there with the intention of observing the crowd gathered to behold it, and I had excellent opportunities of doing so, at intervals all through the night, and continuously from day-break until after the spectacle was over. I believe that a sight so inconceivably awful as the wickedness and levity of the immense crowd collected at that execution this morning could be imagined by no man, and could be presented in no heathen land under the sun. The horrors of the gibbet and of the crime which brought the wretched murderers to it faded in my mind before the atrocious bearing, looks, and language of the assembled spectators. When I came upon the scene at midnight, the shrillness of the cries and howls that were raised from time to time, denoting that they came from a concourse of boys and girls already assembled in the best places, made my blood run cold. As the night went on, screeching, and laughing, and yelling in strong chorus of parodies on negro melodies, with substitutions of 'Mrs. Manning' for 'Susannah', and the like, were added to these. When the day dawned, thieves, low prostitutes, ruffians, and vagabonds of every kind, flocked on to the ground, with every variety of offensive and foul behaviour. Fightings, faintings, whistlings, imitations of Punch, brutal jokes, tumultuous demonstrations of indecent delight when swooning women were dragged out of the crowd by the police, with their dresses disordered, gave a new zest to the general entertainment. When the sun rose brightly–as it did–it gilded thousands upon thousands of upturned faces, so inexpressibly odious in their brutal mirth or callousness, that a man had cause to feel ashamed of the shape he wore, and to shrink from himself, as fashioned in the image of the Devil. When the two miserable creatures who attracted all this ghastly sight about them were turned quivering into the air, there was no more emotion, no more pity, no more thought that two immortal souls had gone to judgement, no more restraint in any of the previous obscenities, than if the name of Christ had never been heard in this world, and there were no belief among men but that they perished like the beasts.

Quite apart from the disgusting spectacle which the gathered crowd made, there was also the purely practical consideration that, if the people were laughing and joking about the awful sight which they were about to witness, then it clearly was not serving the purpose of making them afraid and fearful of falling victim to the same fate. Pickpockets and robbers worked the crowd, literally in the very shadow of the gallows.

When the procession from Newgate arrived at Tyburn, it was to find an atmosphere very similar to a fairground. Food and drink was on sale, people were hawking souvenirs, and the grandstands were full of those who had come to watch the show. Before the hangings began, there would be a chance for the condemned to make speeches. Sometimes these were very affecting, the person about to die having discovered a deep religious belief between sentence and execution. This sort of thing was often viewed with contempt. Even more scorn was reserved for those who deliberately dragged out the process of speech making, either because they were anxious to put off the moment of their execution or in the hope of a reprieve. After all, most of those present had come to watch people die, not listen to a lot of speeches and confessions.

On the other hand, anybody prepared to die with a good natured joke or two was always popular. William Borwick, who had murdered his wife, gave just the sort of speech which everybody enjoyed. He looked dubiously at the rope and gave it a good, hard tug. Turning to the onlookers, he told them with a straight face that he wanted to be sure that the rope was strong enough. After all, he continued with perfect comic timing, if it broke then he might be cast to the ground, break his legs and be crippled for life! This performance was received with a roar of laughter.

There were also moments of high and unexpected drama. Chief among these were last minute reprieves. Although the onlookers had come to see the hanging and experienced a certain measure of disappointment when somebody did not die, reprieves were applauded on the whole.

When hangings began at Tyburn, it was a tiny village several miles outside London; an ideal place to accommodate the noisy crowds and rough behaviour associated with executions. In the rest of the country too, hangings generally took place outside towns, so that there was room for large crowds to gather. It was essential, if the purpose of these exhibitions was to impress the ordinary public, that as many people as possible witnessed the hangings. By the end of the eighteenth century though, cities and towns were growing, not just in population but also in area. The traditional spots for executions began to be encroached upon by the suburbs. This happened in London as well as in other towns.

By 1759, the famous Tyburn 'triple tree' was blocking traffic moving in and out of London from the west of England. It was removed and a new, mobile gallows was used instead; one which could be erected as and when it was needed. This is the gallows upon which Earl Ferrers was hanged in the following year. It was designed so that the condemned person stood on a platform which then fell away, leaving the individual suspended. This developed into the 'new drop' gallows, in which a drop of 2-3ft was arranged. We shall learn more about the advantages and disadvantages of this new method of hanging in Chapter 8.

By the 1780s, not only was Tyburn no longer a country hamlet, it was on the edge of a select, residential district of the largest city on Earth. Those with money were building grand properties on the outskirts of London, and they definitely did not appreciate the crowds who accompanied the procession from Newgate Prison. Those buying stylish and expensive houses in the newly developed districts of Mayfair, Marylebone and Regents Park did not wish to live within earshot of the noisy mobs that frequented the gallows at Tyburn. In 1783, the decision was taken to abandon the practice of conducting executions several miles from prisons and to carry them out in front of the prison walls instead. This practice was quickly adopted in the rest of Britain and within a few years the carnival procession from prisons to gallows had come to an end. Some regretted it, among them Dr Johnson. He remarked petulantly:

> The old method drew together a number of spectators. If they do not draw spectators, they do not answer their purpose. The old method was most satisfactory for all parties: the public was gratified by a procession; the criminal was supported by it. Why has all this to be swept away?

Dr Johnson had hit the nail on the head by observing that if the public executions did not draw spectators, then they did not answer their purpose. He need not have worried though, because the crowds thronging the area around Newgate Prison were no smaller than those which had gathered at Tyburn. A public hanging was still a great attraction.

On 7 November 1783, the last hanging took place at Tyburn when a highwayman called John Austin was executed. Although the decision had actually been taken to halt the executions, following pressure from the wealthy and influential new residents of the district, the move away from Tyburn was presented as being essentially humanitarian in nature; sparing the condemned prisoners the lengthy ordeal of the journey before their deaths. Devotees of hanging in London had only nine days to wait after the abandonment of Tyburn, until the first execution took place in the new location.

On 9 December 1783, enormous crowds gathered outside Newgate Prison to witness both the first execution outside the prison and also a great novelty in the way of hangings – the introduction of a completely new gallows. This was the 'new drop' gallows; a mobile machine which was pulled into position on hanging days by a team of horses. Ten people were hanged simultaneously for the first use of the 'new drop'– nine men and one woman. When the trapdoor was operated, the victims fell 3ft. A few had their necks broken by this fall, but the great majority still died of strangulation. Most prisons adopted versions of the 'new drop' gallows at about this time. Invariably, they were erected either in front of, or in some cases on the roofs of, prisons. As the nineteenth century began, the old custom of the lengthy procession from prison to gallows had stopped entirely.

DRAWING AND QUARTERING:
VARIATIONS ON THE THEME OF HANGING

There was, as we have seen, an established hierarchy of capital punishment in Britain. At the top was the block and axe; when skilfully used, by far and away the most humane and dignified form of execution. Shooting ranked a little lower than this, but was still regarded as an acceptable way to die. Hanging was the death which common criminals faced; there was nothing dignified or noble about kicking out one's life at the end of a rope. Although the underworld tried to make light of it by saying that, 'There's no more to hanging than a wry neck and a wet pair of breeches', the truth was that it was a miserable and degrading death. It was not the worst death to which a man could be sentenced though. There was one type of execution which was reserved for traitors and was universally viewed as a diabolical torment; the most dreadful death which anybody could face.

The purpose of executions, for much of British history, was to strike terror into the hearts of those witnessing them. Treason, being regarded for many centuries as worse than murder, in that it attacked the very social order, was punished in a particularly savage way. In Britain, as in the rest of Europe, a great deal of ingenuity went into devising fiendishly cruel methods of execution for those guilty of regicide, or even attempted regicide.

The killing of a king excited special horror, because it was a crime against the established and God-given order. Consider the case of Robert Damiens who, in 1757, stabbed King Louise XV of France. Although the king did not die, Damiens was subjected to the most appalling death. The hand which had held the knife was burned off in a fire of sulphur, his flesh was torn with red-hot pincers and he was finally dismembered by being pulled apart by four horses, a process which took over three hours.

In Britain, the use of red-hot pincers in this way was almost unknown, but a standard method was eventually worked out, which matched anything on the continent for sheer suffering. Before looking at this method of execution, known popularly as hanging, drawing and quartering, we turn to Scotland to examine a one-off punishment inflicted upon a regicide, a punishment which was even crueller than that endured by Damiens. Scotland seemed to favour some of the more outlandish modes of capital punishment, which were wholly unknown south of the border in England. Breaking on the wheel, for instance, was occasionally carried out in Scotland, but was never recorded in England.

In 1437, a group of conspirators managed to stab to death King James I of Scotland. His wife was a very strong and determined woman and a month after the assassination, she was able to see that the men responsible were brought to justice. Their leader, the Earl of Atholl, was executed over a period of three days. On the first day, he was hoisted by his ankles from a primitive crane and allowed to fall a great distance, before being stopped short by the rope. This wrenched both his legs from their sockets. He was then set in the pillory and an iron crown on which had been inscribed the words 'King of Traitors' was heated in a brazier until it was red hot, before being placed on the wretched Earl's head. The next day, he was brought again to the scaffold and blinded. His flesh was then torn with red-hot pincers. On the third and final day, he was stretched out on a board and his stomach slit open. His internal organs were removed and thrown in a fire. Once he was dead, his head was removed and set up above the city gate.

This ingenious execution contains one feature which was to become a standard part of the familiar punishment of hanging, drawing and quartering; namely, the cutting open of the stomach to pull out various organs. Let us see how this method of execution worked.

To begin with, the victim was drawn to the gallows at the tail of a horse. At one time, this was simply accomplished by dragging the bound man naked through the streets, until the place of execution was reached. The only problem was that after being pulled at speed over a cobbled road, the condemned man was often unconscious or even dead before the execution had even begun. It grew to be the custom in later years to draw the victim on a hurdle. There has been a good deal of debate as to what the 'drawing' part of this execution actually was. Did the word refer to the drawing on a hurdle to execution, or was it a description of a later stage of the process, when the man's intestines were drawn out of his body? To date, there has been no definitive answer to this question. Once the execution ground was reached, the victim would be hanged until he was half dead, although usually still fully conscious.

He would be cut down alive and then castrated. After this, his stomach was cut open and his bowels were pulled out and thrown in a fire. His heart would also be removed and his head cut off. The body would be cut into four parts and the quarters, along with the head, displayed in prominent public locations.

This most disgusting of all modes of capital punishment was reserved exclusively for men found guilty of treason. Women would be burnt at the stake for this offence; it was felt to be indecent to expose a female body publicly to this sort of treatment. The executioner, as a rule, had a certain amount of latitude in the type and degree of pain which he could cause during hanging, drawing and quartering. For instance, he could allow the man to hang until he was completely unconscious or he could, on the other hand, simply suspend him briefly, so that he was completely aware of what was being done to him. The severity of the suffering was sometimes made the subject of an official recommendation. In certain cases, the executioner would be told to hang the man for only a few seconds, long enough to satisfy the letter of the law, but not long enough to cause loss of consciousness. This was to ensure that he would experience the full horrors of this type of death. On other occasions, instructions would be given that the victim should be allowed to hang until he was dead, before the various mutilations were carried out.

The first detailed accounts of hanging, drawing and quartering date from the thirteenth and early fourteenth centuries. One of the earliest cases we know about was the execution of William Wallace, the rebel Scottish leader. By special, royal command, his suffering was as protracted and painful as the hangman could make it, when he met his death at Smithfield on 23 August 1305.

By the time of the Tudors, hanging, drawing and quartering had become a regular entertainment for the crowds. It was regarded as something of a treat for spectators, who were inured to violence by the witnessing of frequent, straightforward and unremarkable hangings. It offered something a little different, calculated to excite the most jaded palate for public death. During the Dissolution of the Monasteries in Henry VIII's reign, any churchman who denied that the King was head of the Church was regarded as being treasonous. A number of abbots and ordinary monks were executed by means of hanging, drawing and quartering. The sentence told the accused:

> That you be drawn on a hurdle to the place of execution where you shall be hanged by the neck and being alive cut down, your privy members shall be cut off and your bowels taken out and burned before you, your head severed from your body and your body divided into four quarters to be disposed of at the King's pleasure.

During Mary's reign, which followed a short time after her father's, religious crimes were punished by burning at the stake. Hundreds of Protestants met their deaths in this way. On the succession of her sister Elizabeth though, there was an abrupt reversal. Elizabeth was a Protestant and declared herself head of the Church in England. It was the turn now of the Catholics to be persecuted. This persecution was undertaken not on religious grounds, but rather the political one of refusing their full allegiance to the monarch. The main targets were priests themselves, rather than Catholics *per se*. Elizabeth had, as she famously said, no desire, 'to make windows into men's souls.' In other words, she did not care if a person was Catholic or Protestant, just so long as he acknowledged her as being head of the Church. This was just what many Catholics could not do.

In 1586, a priest called John Ballard conspired with a group of Catholic gentry, led by Anthony Babington, to launch an insurrection against Queen Elizabeth I. They wanted to install her imprisoned cousin, the Catholic Mary Queen of Scots, on the throne in her place. This was High Treason by any definition, and when the plot was uncovered, those involved expected no mercy. During their trial, when it had become plain that the verdict would be guilty, the Queen enquired if it would be possible for some especially painful death to be devised for these men, so serious was their offence. She spoke at length to Sir William Cecil, Baron Burghley, about this. Since he was one of the commissioners actually trying the case, this was hardly a correct thing to do, but then the Tudor monarchs were never noted for over-adherence to the law. Writing of this conversation later, in a letter to Sir Christopher Hatton, Burghley said that he had explained to Elizabeth that when done efficiently, hanging, drawing and quartering was more terrible than any other sort of execution. This was quite true, as was seen on 20 September 1586, when the first batch of seven conspirators was dispatched at St Giles' Circus, near modern day Tottenham Court Road tube station.

Ballard, the priest, was the first to be executed and the hangman had evidently received very precise instructions. The priest swung for only a moment before he was cut down and dragged to the butcher's block. He was given time to recover his breath, so that he was fully aware of what was going to be done to him, before the mutilation began. His penis and testicles were sliced off and his stomach was cut open. Then the executioner slowly and deliberately began removing his bowels, being careful to try and keep the man alive for as long as possible. Eventually, his heart was removed and his body was dismembered. The other six men were similarly treated. One of them, John Savage, was not even hanged before his ordeal. The rope broke and he was taken at once to the block to be castrated and eviscerated. According to one of the witnesses, William Camden, the men were 'hanged, cut down, their privities cut off, bowelled alive and seeing, and quartered, not without some note of cruelty.' 'Not without some note of cruelty' indicates that these executions were carried out in an especially sadistic fashion.

Even for Elizabethan execution goers, this was a bit much and the crowd showed their disgust at the sickening cruelty which had been used against the condemned men. When Elizabeth was told this, she ordered that the remaining seven who were to be executed the following day, should be left hanging until they were dead, before the butchering was carried out. This gained her a reputation for being merciful and humane; it was not until many years later that it came to light that it was Elizabeth herself who had insisted on the fiendish cruelty used during the execution of the first batch of the Babington plotters.

It is almost impossible to imagine just how gory executions of this kind were, even when the executioner was trying to be merciful to the sufferer. A couple of years before Anthony Babington and his fellow plotters were executed, a Welsh Catholic called Richard White was hanged, drawn and quartered for trying to convert others to Catholicism; which, of course, amounted to treason as the law stood. When he was executed at Wrexham on 15 October 1584, White showed great courage and the crowd was obviously impressed by his speech. He told them, 'I have been a jesting fellow, and if I have offended any that way, or by my songs, I beseech them for God's sake to forgive me.' This was just the sort of thing which people liked to hear and it was plain that it would not be a popular move to let this man undergo the full rigours of the execution. The hangman accordingly allowed White to hang for some time, even hanging on his legs to ensure that he was dead before the mutilations were carried out.

When the hanged man was cut down, and was being taken to the block to have his entrails removed, he began coughing and gasping. It was clear that there had been a miscalculation and that he was going to be butchered alive and conscious. As if this were not bad enough, the hangman proved to be a bungler, with no real idea how to go about the gruesome task which now faced him. He made a small hole in White's stomach and then began to pull out his intestines in little pieces. The spectators were growing restless at seeing White's agony prolonged in this way, and since he showed no signs of being ready to die, the hangman seized the axe which was to be used for cutting the body into quarters and, to quote a contemporary eyewitness, 'he mangled his breast with a butcher's axe to the very chin most pitifully.'

For Protestants, the burnings at the stake, at Smithfield, have a special place in the creation of martyrs. Catholics have a different set of martyrs, dating from a few years later. These men were not burnt at Smithfield, but hanged, drawn and quartered at Tyburn. Some of them have subsequently been beatified and are now acknowledged as saints by the Catholic Church. They died in the main during the reign of Bloody Mary's sister, Elizabeth. Between 1581 and 1603, over 180 Catholics were hanged, drawn and quartered for treason.

We saw in Chapter 2 that the famous Tyburn gallows were erected in 1571. Their first victim was actually only hanged briefly upon them, before being disembowelled and quartered. The triple tree was constructed in May 1571. On 1 June, Dr John Story, formerly Professor of Civil Law at Oxford University, was, in the words of a contemporary witness:

> Drawn upon a hurdle from the Tower of London unto Tyburn, where was prepared for him a new pair of gallows made in a triangular manner.

Dr Story had been quite powerful under Mary, and, after her death, had been arrested for his role in persecuting Protestants. Although he managed to escape, he was later recaptured and charged with High Treason. He was convicted and, on 1 June, hanged briefly before being disembowelled. He recovered consciousness during this process, sat up and struck the executioner a blow round his head.

Elizabeth I was keen to promote the idea that she was a liberal and enlightened monarch, who wished all men and women in her realm to be free to worship God as they wished. The problem was that a number of Catholics thought of her as a heretic, and felt that it would be a praiseworthy act to bring about her deposition from the throne. From Elizabeth's point of view, hunting down and punishing such people was not a matter of religious persecution, but more about tackling rank treason which threatened the state itself.

Many of the Catholics who suffered this dreadful death at Tyburn were priests. We have already seen the case of John Ballard, who was deeply implicated in a plot to assassinate Queen Elizabeth. By most yardsticks, such a man was guilty of treason and by the *mores* of the time deserved to die a traitor's death. Others though, were condemned simply because they had been saying mass. Take the case of one of the most renowned of these Catholic martyrs, St Edmund Campion.

As a young man, Campion studied at Oxford and intended to become a priest. While there, he met Queen Elizabeth and as one of the most brilliant students at that time, he was talked of as being a possible future Archbishop of Canterbury. In his twenties though, he underwent a crisis of conscience and travelled to France and then Rome, becoming a Catholic priest in the process. He then returned to England under a false name, intending to promote the Catholic faith. The problem was that in the Anglican Church the monarch is both head of State and also head of the Church. By denying the religious supremacy of the English queen, Edmund Campion was coming perilously close to denying her one of the attributes of the sovereign under English law.

In 1581, Campion was arrested and taken to the Tower of London. He had a brief interview with the Queen, who offered him a post in the Anglican Church if he would only renounce his Catholicism. He refused to do so and was brutally tortured to obtain the names of any fellow Catholics he knew. On 1 December 1581, he was drawn to Tyburn on a hurdle and hanged, drawn and quartered with two other priests. He was beatified in 1886, and finally canonised in 1970.

Edmund Campion was one of the so-called Forty martyrs of England and Wales; Catholics executed in this country supposedly for treason between 1535 and 1679. Some of these men and women, John Ballard for instance, plainly were guilty of treason, to the extent that they were actively plotting the over-throw or death of the monarch. Others though were guilty of nothing more than refusing to acknowledge the English monarch as head of the Church.

The behaviour of the Catholics who were martyred in this way at Tyburn, often provoked unwilling admiration from the crowd. There were even cases of spectators converting to the Catholic faith as a result of witnessing these brave men being done to death. To counter this, the government began order-ing that Catholics who were to be executed for treason, should die alongside common criminals, who were being hanged for murder and theft. This move proved counter-productive, as in their final speeches, these religious martyrs reminded the crowd that Jesus himself had been executed with thieves.

Near to the spot where these executions took place now stands the Tyburn Convent, in the crypt of which is a model of the triangular gallows. There are also remains of various people hanged, drawn and quartered at Tyburn and subsequently canonised. These include such grisly fragments as a vertebra and a finger bone.

Despite Elizabeth I's famous comment about not wishing to make win-dows into men's souls and being content with outward observance, it is hard to escape the feeling that at least some of these Catholics were hanged, drawn and quartered for their religious beliefs. Indeed, in some cases this was proved by the behaviour of the authorities at their executions.

Take the case of Alban Roe, who was hanged, drawn and quartered in 1642. Before his trial for treason, he had been imprisoned in the Fleet Prison for seventeen years. During the whole of this time, he had ministered to other prisoners and tried to convert them to Catholicism. When his trial was finally held, the verdict was never in doubt. On the scaffold, he was good natured and made several jokes. Noticing one of his former gaolers in the crowd around the scaffold, he told the man, 'Friend, I find that thou art a prophet. Thou hast told me often that I should be hanged.' Roe was allowed to address the crowd, and he used the opportunity to remove any doubt as to the true reason for which he was to be hanged, drawn and quartered. Turning to the sheriff, he asked whether he could even at this last moment save his life by becoming a Protestant. Eagerly, the man confirmed that this was so. He had fallen into a trap. Roe turned back to the crowd, announcing triumphantly that they could 'see then this crime for which I am to die and whether religion be not my only treason?'

As is so often the case when terrible punishments of this sort are inflicted on devoutly religious men, solely because they would not acknowledge the English king or queen as the head of their Church, the result was to provoke sympathy for them. It also engendered curiosity about the cause which would lead such decent people to suffer death in so dreadful a fashion. In fact, a number of Protestants were converted to Catholicism as a direct result of witnessing such executions.

As Britain entered the seventeenth century, hanging, drawing and quartering declined a little in popularity. In 1660 though, following Charles II's restoration to the throne, there was a spate of such executions. Soon after the new king's return to England, a Bill was passed in parliament promising an amnesty for almost everybody who had fought against the Crown during the English Civil War. The exception were those who had been directly concerned in the execution of Charles I; the so-called regicides. Fifty-nine men had signed the King's death warrant and after the restoration, all those who were not dead or who had not had the sense to flee the country, were rounded up and tried for treason. Those convicted were hanged, drawn and quartered. It was clear that the executioner had received instructions that the full horrors of the sentence were to be carried out. The first to be executed was Major General Thomas Harrison, who had made no effort to escape the country because, it was said, he did not expect the new king to seek revenge for his father's death. In this, he was greatly mistaken. Pepys described the scene in his diary:

> I went out to Charing Cross to see Major-General Harrison hanged, drawn and quartered – which was done there – he looking as cheerfully as any man could do in that condition. He was presently cut down and his head and his heart shown to the people, at which there were great shouts of joy.

Samuel Pepys left out some of the details of this, the first execution of those who had had a hand in the death of Charles I. Although some people, like Pepys, admired Major General Harrison's composure, others were sure that he was shaking with fear. One contemporary account says that, 'All the way as he went he endeavoured to discover to the world the undauntedness of his spirit.' Another witness though, noted, 'the more than ordinary trembling and shaking of his joints.' This trembling caused some of the crowd to make jokes and call out sarcastic comments about his apparent cowardice in the face of death. Harrison was so irritated by this that he broke off his speech on the scaffold, claiming that it was an old war wound causing his shaking, not fear.

The condemned man was only allowed to hang for a few seconds before being cut down and disembowelled. He was fully conscious during the procedure, which was proved when at one point, while the executioner was rummaging about in his intestines, he sat up suddenly and hit the man round the head.

Executions of this sort continued for a few more years; in 1681 Oliver Plunkett, Primate of all Ireland, was tried for treason and subsequently hanged, drawn and quartered at Tyburn. He was the last Catholic martyr to die in this country and was later beatified. His mummified head can be found in St Peter's Church in Drogheda. Some of those convicted after the 1715 uprising in Scotland were hanged, drawn and quartered, but by this time all were allowed to hang until they were dead. It was to be almost another century before the last sentence of hanging, drawing and quartering was pronounced.

In 1803, during the Napoleonic Wars, a plot was hatched to assassinate the king and seize control of the Tower of London and Bank of England. The men behind this mad scheme were all tried for treason and sentenced to be hanged, drawn and quartered. This was later commuted to hanging and beheading. An exceedingly gruesome scene took place on the scaffold following the hanging of the seven men, all of whom were allowed to die before any attempt was made to sever their heads. The instigator of the conspiracy, Colonel Edward Despard, was the first to be dealt with. A surgeon tried to remove his head neatly after he had been hanged, by using a scalpel. He was unable to manage this and when he had been fiddling around in this way for some minutes, trying to find the right place to cut through the vertebrae, he was elbowed aside by the hangman. Impatient at this delicate fiddling about, he grabbed hold of the head by the ears and twisted it round a couple of times, wrenching it off by brute force. He then held it aloft and proclaimed the traditional formula, 'Behold the head of Edward Marcus Despard, a traitor!'

The last time that the sentence of hanging, drawing and quartering was carried out was on 28 April 1820, when the Cato Street conspirators were tried. In their case too, it was commuted to hanging and posthumous beheading. It was not quite the last time that such a sentence was passed. Following the so-called Newport Rising in 1839, when 10,000 Chartists fought pitched battles with the army, exchanging shots in the streets with the troops, three ringleaders were charged with High Treason. Their trial was held at the Monmouth Shire Hall, and on 16 January 1840, all three were sentenced to be hanged, drawn and quartered. Following extensive lobbying of the government in London, these sentences were later commuted to transportation for life to Australia. The penalty remained on the Statute Book until 1870, when it was removed by the passage of the Forfeiture Act.

THE NINETEENTH CENTURY: THE BIRTH OF MODERN HANGING

8

We have seen that some of those hanged by the old methods managed to grant themselves a swift and relatively painless death, by leaping off ladders and carts by their own volition and breaking their necks. This was a chancy business, because sometimes the rope broke and the whole thing would have to be endured a second time. There was, in any case, no guarantee of breaking one's neck by this means; it was very much the luck of the draw.

In 1759, a new type of gallows was tried out, which entailed the condemned person standing on a platform which was then removed. This led to the development of the so-called 'short drop', which was thought by many to be an improvement on the old method. Whereas the experimental gallows upon which Earl Ferrers died in 1760 had a drop of only a few inches, the 'short drop', otherwise known as the 'new drop', increased this to 2–3ft. Sometimes this was sufficient to break the neck; although most victims still struggled and choked on the end of the rope. This new technique was widely adopted throughout the whole of Britain.

Although it was, at first, thought that the new method of hanging would be more humane and so would ensure a speedier and less painful death, this did not always appear to be the case. The drop of 2–3ft often stunned the victim, but seldom killed them outright. The death agonies of those being hanged in this way appeared to spectators to be no less agonising than those suffered by people turned off ladders or tipped out of carts. A few examples will indicate how these new hangings were operating in the early years of the nineteenth century.

In 1802, the former governor of the British colony of Gorée was hanged for the murder of a British soldier. We shall look at the events leading up to this execution in Chapter 10, but for now it is enough to note that this elderly man took fifteen minutes to die, struggling convulsively on the end of the rope for the whole time. Two executions, that took place a few years later, showed that the 'short drop' technique left a lot to be desired.

John Ashton was a highwayman who had been sentenced to death. On 22 August 1814 he was hanged, but not without the crowd outside Newgate Prison being entertained even more than was usual. Since his trial, Ashton had apparently gone completely mad. Whether or not he had been driven mad by the strain of being under sentence of death or whether he had been a little touched beforehand is not known, but the fact is, he behaved in an extraordinary fashion. When his irons were being struck off, he pulled grotesque faces and gibbered. Once on the scaffold, he began dancing and capering and singing, 'I'm Lord Wellington!'

Ashton would not stand still for the customary prayers and had to be held in place by two guards, to prevent him from disrupting the ceremony entirely. All this was hugely popular with the onlookers, who shouted their appreciation and roared with laughter at his antics. This was only the prelude. He was to be hanged with five other men and when they had all been lined up on the drop, the signal was given and they fell 3ft. At this point, an incredible thing happened. John Ashton bounced back up again and managed to get his feet back onto the scaffold. He then began dancing again, crying out, 'What do you think of me? Am I not Lord Wellington now?' The flustered executioner then rushed round and pushed him back over the drop. He did not emerge again.

If the execution of John Ashton did not demonstrate that the 'short drop' was flawed, then the case of Mary Green, hanged for counterfeiting in 1819, surely did. On 22 March, she was hanged, being left to hang for a while after the execution. When she was cut down, she showed signs of life and, in fact, recovered and went on to live to a ripe old age.

Because of the way the gallows were now constructed, many of the shortcomings of the 'short drop' were not immediately apparent to those watching on. The victims fell into a box-like structure made of wood, in which they were hidden from view. It became customary for the hangman to descend into this space and hang on the legs of those he had hanged, if they were struggling or showing signs of life. This is the origin of the expression 'pulling one's leg', to indicate a sham. To this extent at least, the new arrangement was an improvement. Nobody could actually see the hanged men and women kicking their legs and fighting for breath.

It was with the introduction of gallows of this kind, that it became routine to pull a hood over the heads of those about to be hanged, and to tie their ankles together. The original purpose of covering the face was to spare spectators the sight of the blackened and congested faces of those choking to death. When the drop was adopted, it became more important to prevent those about to be hanged from being able to gauge the precise moment that the trapdoor was about to open. If they knew this, then there might have been a temptation to jump off the drop at the crucial moment.

A word needs to be said, at this point, about the type of nooses used during hangings in this country. For most people, the idea of hanging evokes an image of the traditional 'cowboy's coil'– a noose tied with an elaborate knot topped with a dozen coils of rope. This is the kind of noose which we see in westerns, and it is associated in the popular mind with gallows and hanging. As a matter of fact, this type of noose was seldom employed in British executions. The problem with a 'cowboy coil' is that it tends to be stiff, and not free running at all. In order to break the neck cleanly, it is not enough simply to have a long drop. The noose must snap tight with great force and thus fracture the spine. This, in theory, causes instant loss of consciousness and rapid death. The most effective way of achieving this is to have a knot with a loop at one end of the rope, and to pass the rope through this, making a loose, running knot. By the end of the Victorian era, the end of the rope was woven firmly into a brass eyelet, through which the other end of the rope was simply threaded.

After many decades of the Bloody Code, it was clear to everybody that such harsh punishments were doing nothing to address the crime rate. In addition to this, the sight of mass hangings in the centre of cities was becoming incompatible with the civilised society into which Britain was turning. In 1823, the Judgement of Death Act was passed. This made the death sentence mandatory for only two offences – murder and treason. From then on, judges could decide whether to sentence a convicted criminal to death, or to substitute a lesser penalty such as transportation or prison. The previous year had seen the last execution for shoplifting in this country, and from 1823 onwards, the number of executions fell dramatically. In 1829, the last person was hanged for forgery. In the following years hanging for offences, other than murder, gradually fell out of favour.

Further Acts, in the course of the 1830s, reduced the number of capital crimes to just sixteen. The Criminal Law Consolidation Act of 1861 reduced the number of capital offences to just four – murder, High Treason, piracy and arson in the Royal Dockyards. That same year saw the last execution for attempted murder take place at Chester.

For much of the nineteenth century, William Calcraft was the most notable hangman in the country. He began carrying out executions in 1829 and continued for an astonishing forty-five years, until he was too decrepit to continue with the work. Calcraft was the first hangman to travel around the country by railway, which meant that rather than being the London hangman, he was effectively the hangman for the entire country. Public hanging was as popular in the mid-nineteenth century as ever it had been during the days of Tyburn. The new railway companies laid on special excursion trains to towns where a hanging was being held. Tourists flocked to such events. It was not uncommon to find a crowd of 20,000 waiting outside a prison to witness the grisly ritual of public execution.

Some executions were better value for the spectators than others. The execution of William Bousfield, which took place outside Newgate Prison on 31 March 1856, was one of these – an execution to be relished by the macabre connoisseurs of such things.

William Bousfield was a twenty-nine-year-old tobacconist in London. He had a wife and three children, of whom he seemed to be tired. In the early hours of 3 February 1856, Bousfield turned up at Bow Street police station. He was dripping with blood and calmly told the officer on duty that he had killed his wife. When the police went to his home, they found that not only had he cut his wife's throat with a razor, but that he had also stabbed all three of his children to death with a chisel.

Matters moved very swiftly and on 6 March, Bousfield appeared at the Old Bailey, charged with four counts of murder. The case was so open and shut that the jury did not even retire before bringing in a verdict of guilty. At this, Bousfield fainted. He was taken to Newgate Prison to await execution. Whilst there, he constantly complained about the injustice of his sentence, claiming that the crimes had been committed in a moment of madness and that it was unfair to punish him for this.

On 29 March, two days before he was due to die, Bousfield's sisters visited him in prison. Once they left, he suddenly dived at the fire, burning in the hearth and plunged his head into it, in an apparent suicide attempt. He was restrained and the doctor was called. Bousfield was patched up as best as could be done. From then, until the day of his execution, he neither spoke nor ate anything. On the morning of 31 March, when Calcraft came to pinion him, Bousfield's pulse was so weak that the doctor feared that he might die before he was hanged. The condemned man was slumped in a chair, seemingly unable to move at all. He was carried onto the scaffold and seated in a chair while the noose was fitted.

William Calcraft, something of a bungler at the best of times was particularly nervous that day, due to having received a death threat. Specifically, he had been warned that he would be shot while on the scaffold. Had he been in a calmer frame of mind, then it might have occurred to him that allowing Bousfield to be hanged while sitting would reduce the drop to almost nothing.

As soon as he operated the drop, Calcraft darted back into the prison, clearly scared of being shot. There were cries of amazement from the crowd, because Bousfield had somehow recovered consciousness and managed to hook his legs onto the scaffold, and thus pulled himself out of the pit. A prison warder dashed round and pushed him off again. The impetus of this allowed him to swing to the other side of the scaffold and he managed to get his feet over the edge and haul himself up again. Calcraft was sent for and the hanging man was once more pushed off the scaffold, but once again he succeeded in getting his legs hooked over the edge of the trap. Calcraft went below and seized hold of the struggling man and hung on until Bousfield died of strangulation. Following this execution, it became the practice to strap the condemned man's ankles together on the drop, in order to prevent anything of the sort happening again.

Scenes such as those that took place during William Bousfield's execution provided ammunition for those who wanted to put an end to the practice of public hanging. It served only to provide gruesome entertainment, and did not fulfil any practical function beyond that. Nobody even paid lip service to the fiction that public displays of this kind discouraged crime. Even so, it was to be over ten years before public executions in this country finally came to an end.

Some of the biggest crowds ever seen at hangings gathered outside Newgate during the 1860s. In 1864, the *Flowery Land* mutineers, seamen who had murdered the captain of their ship, were hanged. One estimate was that 200,000 people assembled for the hanging of the five men. Even taking into account the fact that this is very probably an exaggeration, the actual number must still have been many thousands.

In 1867, the British were troubled by a forerunner of the IRA, the Irish Republican Brotherhood. They were more commonly known as the Fenians. When two of them were arrested in London and remanded to the Clerkenwell House of Detention, a prison near Farringdon Road, their comrades devised an audacious escape plan. This entailed blowing up the walls of the prison's exercise yard, so that the two imprisoned men could make a run for it. It was a mad scheme and it was, in retrospect, inevitable that it should have miscarried.

On the afternoon of 13 December 1867, a group of men pushed a hand-barrow through the streets of Clerkenwell. On it was perched a beer barrel containing a quarter of a ton of gunpowder. This was set down by the prison wall and the fuse was lit. The resulting explosion was heard 30 miles away and devastated the surrounding area. Hundreds of houses were damaged and twelve people were killed.

The man who lit the fuse, an Irishman called Michael Barrett, was arrested in Glasgow and was brought back to London for trial. At the same time as Barrett's trial, Parliament was debating a new piece of legislation which would put an end to public hangings forever. The Capital Punishment Amendment Act received the Royal Assent on 29 May 1868. Three days earlier, Michael Barrett had become the last person to be publicly hanged in Britain.

William Calcraft was now an old man, and there was increasing concern about the suffering caused to criminals by the 'short drop', which by that time had been in regular use for almost a century. Two things were plain. First, that it was high time Calcraft was pensioned off, and a new and more efficient hangman engaged. Secondly, there was an urgent need for a new way of carrying out executions – one which would cause instantaneous death.

As is so often the case with major scientific discoveries, two men in different countries simultaneously hit upon a revolutionary idea, in this case a new technique for painless hanging. Just as Charles Darwin and Alfred Wallace both came up with the idea of evolution at the same time, or both Leibniz and Newton devised calculus independently, so too the 'long drop' method of hanging was devised by two men at the same time. In Ireland, the drops given during hanging were considerably longer than those favoured by the English. When Patrick Kilkenny was hanged in Dublin in 1865, for instance, he was given a drop of 14ft – five or six times as long as Calcraft was in the habit of giving. A clergyman, Revd Samuel Haughton, was intrigued by this problem, and came up with the idea that the length of the drop should be related to the weight of the victim. In 1866, Revd Haughton contributed an article to the *London, Edinburgh and Dublin Philosophical Magazine and Journal of Science*. In this piece, entitled 'On hanging, considered from a mechanical and physiological point of view', he expounded his theory that the correct drop needed to break the neck cleanly could be gauged by dividing the weight of the condemned person in pounds, by 2,240. This would give the length of the drop in feet.

While Revd Haughton was contributing his ideas to learned journals, another, more practical man was also giving the matter a good deal of thought. William Marwood was a cobbler in the Linclonshire town of Horncastle, and he had a great interest in hanging. He had independently come up with a similar idea to Samuel Haughton's, and he began badgering the governors of various prisons for a chance to try out his method. Eventually, the fifty-four-year-old shoemaker, who had never assisted at or even witnessed an execution, was invited to carry out the hanging of Frederick Horry. On 31 March 1872, Marwood arrived at Lincoln Prison and prepared the gallows in readiness for the next day. The execution went off without a hitch, and there was none of the twitching, writhing and gasping for breath which were so common with the 'short drop'. The governor of Lincoln Prison recommended William Marwood, and so when Calcraft was retired with a pension in 1874, Marwood was appointed the official hangman for London and Middlesex.

The 'long drop' was being used by all prisons in 1875. Marwood calculated each drop on an individual basis, but this led to problems in the future. Although none of his 'clients' had this misfortune, after Marwood's death, James Berry took over as hangman and he managed to remove the heads of more than one person, by giving too long a drop. It was a fine line to tread. On the one hand, one wished to break the neck instantly, but at the same time, one did not wish to decapitate the victim entirely. On the other hand, nobody wanted to see any more short drops, which left people gasping and struggling for fifteen minutes on the end of a rope. Following some particularly ghastly hangings, such as the 'Goodale Mess', at which we looked in Chapter 1, a commission was set up to standardise the way that the drop was calculated for hangings. It was chaired by Lord Abedare and it began sitting in 1886.

The aim of hanging with the long drop is to deliver a striking force of around a thousand foot-pounds to between either the second and third, or fourth and fifth cervical vertebrae. This will rupture the spinal cord and cause unconsciousness and, usually, immediate death. To achieve this end, it is necessary, in fact vital, to position the noose so that the knot is under the left side of the jaw. This means that when it tightens, it ends up beneath the chin, throwing the head back sharply and fracturing the vertebrae. The Capital Sentences Committee, to give the Abedare Committee its correct name, was set up because there had been a good deal of bad publicity about the conduct of executions. Bartholomew Binns, the hangman who first succeeded William Marwood, was plainly drunk during at least two or three of the dozen or so executions which he conducted. Not only this, but he spent the evenings preceding executions in various pubs, showing off the rope which he would be using to hang a man the next day. This brought the whole business of hanging into disrepute. Berry was a little better, although he was still in the habit of selling on the ropes to souvenir hunters after executions. Another problem with James Berry was a little more serious though, and it led to the establishment of the Abedare Committee.

Berry was not a bungler like Calcraft and certainly did not routinely choke his victims to death, rather than breaking their necks humanely. On the other hand, an awful lot of his hangings did seem to go wrong in one way or another. Sometimes this was not his fault, as in the case of John Lee, 'The man they could not hang', whose execution was unable to take place at Exeter in 1885. We shall look in more detail at this case in Chapter 13, but it is enough for now to observe that, although hooded and noosed upon the drop, it proved impossible to operate the trapdoors and actually hang Lee. This created a sensation in the British press at the time. Worse still were the occasions when Berry managed to behead the men he was hanging. Although this was not a common occurrence, it happened often enough to make people uneasy. Such instances were caused by the condemned man being given too long a drop.

The suggestion was made during the meeting of the Aberdare Committee, that James Berry was in the habit of increasing the length of drops far beyond what was generally thought wise. Much mention was made, during one session of the committee, about the execution of Thomas Currell, which took place on 18 April 1887. The Aberdare Committee met for two years and so was able to examine cases almost as they took place.

The execution of Thomas Currell was notable for several reasons. In the first place, Berry supplemented his income by taking 'assistants' to the hangings – people who paid him for the experience. This happened on the occasion of Currell's execution and was widely known. Secondly, the drop which Berry actually gave Currell was far longer than the one he had told the prison doctor that he was going to give. He had told the doctor that he would give a drop of 5ft, but on the scaffold, one of the warders whispered to the doctor that in fact the drop Berry was giving was more like 7ft. This proved to be the case and although the cause of death was dislocation of the neck, the blood vessels in the neck were all ruptured, causing blood to gush from the hanged man's mouth.

The prison doctor, Dr Marshall, was appalled at the events of Currell's execution and talked feelingly to the committee about his views, intimating that Berry was not to be trusted to make the necessary calculations.

It also happened that Berry miscalculated in the other direction, giving so short a drop that the executed man died of asphyxiation. Dr Marshall mentioned an execution which he had attended where this had also happened. Again, he attributed it to Berry's inability to work out the best drop. The execution took place in Gloucester on 15 June 1886. Dr Marshall said:

> I descended immediately into the pit where I found the pulse beating at the rate of 80 to the minute and the wretched man struggling desperately to get his hands and arms free. I came to this conclusion from the intense muscular action in the arms, forearms and hands, contractions, not continuous but spasmodic, not repeated with any regularity but renewed in different directions and with desperation. From these signs I did not anticipate a placid expression on the face and I regret to say my fears were correct. On removing the white cap about one and a half minutes after the fall I found the eyes starting from the sockets and the tongue protruded, the face exhibiting unmistakable evidence of intense agony.

Of the twenty-three executions examined by the Aberdare Committee, two had resulted in decapitation and three in strangulation. When the final report was produced, the committee published a table of drops to which all executioners should adhere. This was all well and good, but there was nothing to compel a hangman actually to keep to these recommendations.

A few months after the Aberdare Committee published its report, Robert Upton was hanged at Oxford for the murder of his wife. The medical officer at the prison noticed that, although Berry told him that he would give a drop of 5ft, the actual drop was closer to 7ft. The jury at the inquest, which was held that same day, had heard rumours that something had gone wrong at the execution and insisted on the coffin being opened so that they could examine the dead man for themselves; when the lid of the coffin was removed, those nearby recoiled in horror.

Upton's head was barely attached to his body. The spinal cord had been severed, as had the gullet and windpipe. The head was only hanging on by a thin strip of skin and muscle. It was a miracle that it had not come off entirely.

Other recommendations of the Aberdare Committee were adopted and made mandatory. In fact, some were still in force up until the abolition of hanging in 1964. In order to avoid the unedifying sight of the hangman frequenting public houses on the night before a hanging, and exhibiting his equipment, a rule was introduced that the hangman and his assistant had to arrive at the prison on the day before an execution, at four o'clock in the afternoon. It was also hoped that this would prevent any hangman appearing on the scaffold drunk, as had happened on more than one occasion with Bartholomew Binns. The clothes of the hanged man would from then on be burnt, and were no longer regarded as a perk of the hangman. This too was intended to prevent an unwholesome trade in macabre souvenirs.

In addition to this, all hangmen and assistants were to be approved by the Home Office. This would put an end to the sort of activity which James Berry was fond of, taking substantial payment to allow morbid sightseers the opportunity not only to witness, but even participate in an execution. One man who paid Berry for this experience was the baronet Sir Claude Champion de Crespigny. He assisted Berry at several executions and it became something of a scandal. On one occasion, when Berry turned up at a prison to carry out an execution, the governor warned him about bringing a genuine assistant with him rather than some macabre thrill seeker. He told Berry, 'We don't want any baronets here!'

We have seen that in the past, mass hangings were not uncommon in this country; in 1649, twenty-four people were hanged simultaneously at Tyburn. Even after the introduction of the 'new drop' gallows outside Newgate Prison, eight or ten executions could be carried out at once. This practice declined over the course of the nineteenth century, until two, or three people at most, were hanged at the same time. The last triple execution was carried out in this country in 1896. It was a curious occasion for several reasons, not least because one of those being hanged that day was in good enough spirits to make a joke about the event!

In the early hours of 14 February 1896, two men broke into the home of seventy-nine-year-old Henry Smith, a wealthy man living in the London suburb of Muswell Hill. He was badly beaten and tied up. His house was then

ransacked, but the unfortunate Mr Smith died of his injuries almost immediately. The burglars were tracked down and found to have joined a circus,
which was then travelling in the West Country. They were Albert Milsom and
Henry Fowler. Fowler, a giant of a man, was working as the circus strong man
and he resisted arrest so ferociously that the police ended up knocking him
unconscious.

The Milsom and Fowler case has gone down in legal history as the most
spectacularly unsuccessful example ever of the use of a so-called 'cut-throat
defence'. In this tactic, two men accused of a murder each try and lay the
blame for the crime at the door of the other. The usual result of this is that
both are then convicted; juries typically deciding that there is nothing to
choose between the pair. As soon as he was arrested, Milsom admitted that he
had burgled the house in Fowler's company, but claimed that it was Fowler
who had killed the old man and that he himself was quite blameless. When
Fowler first heard Milsom's allegation, which was when they were sitting
side-by-side in the dock at the Old Bailey, he attacked him, trying to throttle
Milsom to death.

As generally happens in cases such as this, the jury decided that both men
were equally culpable, and Mr Justice Hawkins sentenced both to death.
Milsom broke down at this point, sobbing with terror. Fowler just laughed as
he was sentenced to hang and gave a contemptuous imitation of the wretched
Milsom's moans.

Both men were removed to Newgate Prison to await execution. Something
of a backlog was building up at Newgate; there were four people lying under
sentence of death there. One of them was Amelia Dyer, a woman convicted
of the murder of a baby for whom she was caring. The other was William
Seaman, another burglar who had murdered the occupants of the house he
was robbing. The original plan was to hang all four at the same time, resulting
in the first quadruple execution seen at Newgate for some years. At the last
moment, this plan was abandoned. It was thought that it would be too terrible for a woman to hang in this way as part of a job-lot, multiple execution.
On the morning of the execution, Mrs Dyer was, without any explanation,
bundled into a prison van and driven through the streets for a while until the
three men had been hanged.

On the morning of 9 June 1896, Milsom and Fowler paid the ultimate
penalty for their crime. There was a fear that Fowler might disrupt the execution by trying to attack Milsom again, if he found himself next to his former
mate on the scaffold. A plan was devised to prevent this. Milsom was brought
to the gallows first and then William Seaman was placed next to him. When
Fowler was brought in, he was to be placed next to Seaman. It was hoped that
this would allow the hanging to take place without any unpleasantness. Only
when Milsom and Seaman were standing on the drop, hooded and noosed,

was Fowler brought in. He at once asked whether or not Milsom was there, being unable to recognise either of the men present because of the white hoods covering their heads. On being told that Milsom was also about to die, Fowler expressed his satisfaction. Seaman, unaware until this moment of the reason for all the fuss about making sure that he stood in a certain spot on the scaffold, remarked loudly and jocularly from beneath the hood, 'Well this is the first time in my life I've been a bloody peacemaker!' A moment later, all three men were dead.

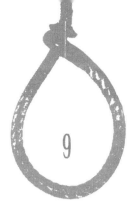

9

LESSER KNOWN METHODS
OF BRITISH EXECUTION:
CRUSHING, BREAKING AND BOILING TO DEATH

So far, we have looked at various methods of execution which are likely to be familiar in varying degrees to readers. We know that hanging was used in this country, as well as burning, shooting and beheading. Most people, similarly, have heard of being hanged, drawn and quartered. How many, though, will have heard of breaking on the wheel, pressing to death or being boiled alive as techniques of capital punishment in Britain? It is time to explore some of the more outlandish forms of execution from this country's past.

We shall begin with breaking on the wheel. Widely used on the continent, there can be few more painful ways to die. The condemned man or woman was tied spread-eagled to either a large cartwheel, or a cross made from lengths of timber. The executioner would then use either an iron bar or perhaps simply a hammer, to smash all the limbs in two places. The shins and thighs would be broken, followed by the upper and lower arms. What happened next depended upon the nature of the crime for which the person was suffering. If it was a straightforward murder, then the individual might be killed, as soon as the arms and legs had been broken, with either a blow to the heart or by strangulation. This strangulation was known as the *retentum*, and a court could decide beforehand how long the person should be allowed to suffer, before being given the merciful release of death. One or two hours were typical. This form of execution lingered on in Europe until the mid-nineteenth century; the last case being in Prussia in 1841, when the man who assassinated the Bishop of Ermeland was broken on the wheel.

Breaking on the wheel was never used in England, but there are one or two cases of its being used in Scotland. In 1591, John Dickson was convicted of parricide, the murder of his father. He faced excommunication for this offence, and apparently lied about it during the ceremony, which might perhaps account for his being one of only a handful of people sentenced to this terrible death. He was broken on the evening of 30 April 1591, and then left to suffer all night long, being finally killed the following day; his corpse was then hanged from a gibbet.

There is only one other recorded case of breaking on the wheel in Scotland. On 2 July 1600, John Kinkaid was murdered by his wife; she was assisted by a servant called Robert Weir. A female servant was also in on the plot. This sort of crime, where servants killed their master, was regarded as being particularly loathsome – on a par with treason. The wife was beheaded and the female servant burnt, but Robert Weir escaped and was not apprehended for another three years. When he was caught, he was executed by being tied to a cart wheel and having his arms and legs smashed with the coulter of a plough. These are the only cases of breaking on the wheel of which we know.

The idea of criminals being boiled alive in a cauldron has an Arabian Nights flavour to it, and it is difficult to believe that this punishment was specifically prescribed in Tudor law for cases of poisoning. In 1531, a man called Richard Roose managed to poison the food in the kitchen of the Bishop of Rochester. The bishop did not die, but because he was in the habit of distributing food to the poor people of Rochester, the crime had the unexpected consequence of killing an old woman who was begging alms of the Bishop's household. A member of the Bishop's staff also died. When news of this crime reached London, it was assumed that it was primarily an attempt on the life of the Bishop himself – a heinous crime indeed. It was announced that the law was to be changed, and that such cases were in the future to be treated as treason, although with a very special and apposite punishment. The poison had been added to cooked food – therefore the perpetrators of such crimes should themselves be cooked.

The contemporary account of the crime reads, with the quaint spelling suitably modernised, as follows:

One Richard Roose late of Rochester in the county of Kent, otherwise called Richard Coke, of his most wicked and damnable disposition did cast a certain venom or poison into a vessel replenished with yeast or balm standing in the kitchen of the Reverend Father in God John, Bishop of Rochester at his palace in Lambeth Marsh, with which yeast or balm and other things convenient porridge or gruel was forthwith made for his family there being, whereby not only the number of eighteen persons of his said family which did eat of that porridge were mortally infected and poisoned, and one of them, that is to say, Benett Curwen, gentleman thereof is deceased, but also certain poor people which resorted to the said Bishop's palace and were there charitably fed with the remains of the said porridge and other victuals, were likewise infected, and one poor woman of them, that is to say, Alyce Tryppytt, widow, is also thereof now deceased: our said Sovereign Lord the King, of his blessed disposition inwardly abhorring all such abominable offences because that in manner no person can live in safety out of danger of death by that means of practise thereof should not be eschewed, hath ordained and enacted by authority of this present parliament that the said poisoning be adjudged and deemed as high-treason. And that the said Richard Roose for the said murder and poisoning of the said two persons as is aforesaid by authority of this present parliament shall stand and be attainted of high-treason: And by cause that detestable offence now newly practised and committed requires condign punishment for the same; It is ordained and enacted by authority of this present parliament that the said Richard Roose shall be therefore boiled to death without having any advantage of his clergy. And that from henceforth every wilful murder of any person or persons by any whatsoever person or persons hereafter to be committed and done by means or way of poisoning shall be reputed, deemed, and judged in the law to be high treason; And that all and every person or persons which hereafter shall be lawfully indicted, appealed and attainted or condemned of such treason for any manner of poisoning shall not be admitted to the benefit of his or their clergy, but shall be immediately committed to execution of death by boiling for the same.

On 5 April 1531, this terrible sentence was carried out and Roose was boiled to death in a large cauldron at Smithfield. He was placed in the water when it was cold and it took so long to heat the cauldron, that it was two hours before he died. That same year, a maid was boiled to death in the market place at Kings Lynn for poisoning her mistress.

This form of execution typically took a couple of hours to kill the victim. The condemned person would be trussed up, unable to move, and then placed up to their necks in a large container of cold water. A fire was lit underneath and the water was brought to the boil. A different method was used for the execution in Kings Lynn. On that occasion, the water was first made boiling hot and the woman was suspended above it from a rope. She was repeatedly dipped into the water and then drawn out again. Local legend has it that she died when the heat caused her chest to burst open, and her heart flew out and struck the wall of a nearby building. A brick in the wall of a house in the market place has a heart carved into it to commemorate this.

On 28 March 1542, another maid was boiled to death at Smithfield for poisoning members of the household where she was living. In 1547, after Henry VIII's son Edward had come to the throne, the Act was repealed. This was done by a passing a statute which abolished all new definitions of treason enacted over the previous decades. There is a curious legal problem posed by the execution of Richard Roose in this way. Because the law of treason was mended only after his arrest, it has been supposed that he was the victim of a retroactive law; something which has always been viewed with disfavour in this country. However, records from 1522, nine years before Roose was executed, make mention of somebody being 'sodden in a cauldron at Smithfield' for 'attempting to poison diverse persons.' It seems that this punishment was already in use before Richard Roose committed the crime for which he died. It has to be borne in mind that poisoning has always been seen as a particularly loathsome crime, and even today when a person is accused of murder by this means, it is customary for the Attorney General to prosecute in person, as a mark of the seriousness with which poisoning is regarded.

Breaking on the wheel and boiling to death were curiosities, only used on one or two occasions. Pressing to death, however, was in constant use up until the eighteenth century. It was a desperately painful death, far worse than hanging, and yet a number of people voluntarily chose to endure it, rather than being hanged. We shall see why this was later.

The procedure for pressing to death was simple and brutal. The prisoner was stretched out on his or her back, with ropes around the ankles and wrists. These were secured to posts or rings in a wall, so that the person was unable to move. A door or wooden board was placed on the person's chest and weights were piled onto it until death resulted. It was possible to extend the process by putting enough weight on the victim to cause great agony, but not enough to cause death.

Under what circumstances was pressing to death used? The official name for this process is *Peine forte et Dure*, which translates from the Norman French, very roughly, as 'hard and strong prison'. This procedure was officially sanctioned in 1275, for those who refused to be tried by 'the Law of the Realm'. It was inflicted upon those who were accused of a felony, but who refused to plead either guilty or not guilty to the charge; to use the legal expression, they were 'mute of malice'. In the beginning, when the problem first cropped up of prisoners who refused to plead at their trial, the sentence of 'hard and strong prison' meant just that. They were taken off and locked up in a small cell with minimal comforts, until they changed their minds. Some people though, can be exceedingly obstinate and it was found that prisoners might be happy to wait it out until the judge had given up. So, it was that the recognised form of the *Peine forte et Dure* was devised to speed things up a little. This type of persuasion, pressing under heavy weights, was definitely in use by 1406. There were actually two very different ways of applying the *Peine forte et Dure*. In the first instance, it was used to persuade the accused person to plead to a charge. In other words, it was a way literally to put pressure upon somebody to do as expected. As soon as the individual complied, he or she would be released and the trial could begin as normal – once a plea had been entered. On other occasions, the *Peine forte et Dure* was used as a punishment in itself. Even if the person, who had previously been refusing to plead, then spoke out, it was too late. The crushing to death continued.

Why would anybody choose to endure this terrible death? The answer was simple. Those convicted of a capital offence forfeited all their estate to the Crown. If a man was convicted say, of treason, then the Crown would seize everything he owned after his execution. This would leave his family penniless. If however he died without being convicted, then the Crown had no more claim upon his estate than if he had been found innocent. There were other advantages for those who refused to plead. Let us look at the case of Margaret Clitheroe, pressed to death in York in 1586, to see another reason for refusing to plead.

Margaret Clitheroe was an ardent Catholic who, during the reign of Elizabeth I, sheltered Catholic priests at her home in the Shambles, a street in York. This was a hazardous undertaking, as it was technically treason to do so. In early 1586, she was arrested and brought before the York Assizes, charged with harbouring priests. She was a married woman with three children and it was this which caused her to decide not to plead to the charge against her. She feared, probably correctly, that if a trial was held, then her children would be called as witnesses. If they refused to give evidence against their mother, then they too could find themselves in trouble, possibly even being tortured to extract information. She was also concerned about her servants, in the event that she was brought to trial.

Margaret Clitheroe must have known full well the consequences of refusing to plead in a case such as this. On 25 March, which also happened to be Good Friday, she was stretched out on her back, with a sharp stone, the size of a man's fist, beneath her back. This was actually a merciful variation to the procedure, and was intended to break her back or puncture her ribs and stop her heart fairly swiftly. A door was then placed over her and over 800lbs of stone and iron were placed on it. She was dead within fifteen minutes.

Margaret Clitheroe was later canonised and is now a saint of the Catholic Church. Her house in the Shambles is still standing, and a nearby convent has in its possession a gruesome relic. Her body was thrown onto a rubbish heap after her death, but a Catholic sympathiser cut off her hand as a memento of the affair. It can still be seen in a glass bell jar at the Bar Convent in York. The words of the sentence for the use of *Peine forte et Dure* are chilling:

> That the prisoner should be sent to the prison from whence he came, and put into a mean room, stopped from the light, and shall there be laid on the bare ground, without any litter, straw, or other covering, or without any garment about him, except something to hide his privy members. He shall lie upon his back; his head shall be covered and his feet shall be bare. One of his arms shall be drawn with a cord to one side of the room, and the other arm to the other side, and his legs shall be served in the like manner. Then there shall be laid upon his body as much iron or stone as he can bear, and more. And the first day after he shall have three morsels of barley bread, without any drink; and the second day he shall be allowed to drink as much as he can at three times of the water that is next the prison door, except running water, without any bread; and this shall be his diet till he dies.

We can see how effective the *Peine forte et Dure* was, by looking at a typical case where it was used to persuade men to enter a plea. In 1723, two highwaymen, thirty-three-year-old Thomas Philips and twenty-seven-year-old William Spigott, were charged with robbery with violence – a hanging offence. They both refused to plead. When they were taken to the press room at Newgate Prison, Philips changed his mind and chose to plead. Since the sentence had already been read, he could still have been quite legally crushed to death, but was allowed to return to the court and stand his trial. Spigott was made of sterner stuff though, and was stripped and stretched upon his back. A weight of over 350lbs was piled onto him and he still refused to plead. Finally, as another 50lbs were about to be added to the pile already pressing him down, he changed his mind and decided to stand trial. Both men were found guilty and were later hanged.

It will be noticed that in the words of the sentence above, there is nothing said about the victim being brought back to plead in court, even if he changed his mind after the pressing had begun. It simply states that the procedure would be carried out until the prisoner died. This was the strict letter of the law, but it was seldom applied. In practice, once the man being pressed indicated that he wished to plead; the ordeal was brought to an end. Sometimes, however, the business was continued to the bitter end, even if the prisoner did change his mind. Such a case occurred in Ireland in 1740. At the Kilkenny Assizes that year, Mathew Ryan stood accused of highway robbery. When he was brought into court and asked how he pleaded, he remained silent. In fact, he had remained silent for the whole time that he had been held after his arrest. His strategy was to pretend to be deaf and dumb. An eyewitness takes up the story:

The judges on this desired the prisoner to plead, but he still pretended to be insensible to all that was said to him. The law called for the *Peine forte et Dure*, but the judges compassionately deferred awarding it until a future day, in the hope that he might in the meantime acquire a juster sense of his situation. When again brought up, however, the criminal persisted in his refusal to plead: and the court at last pronounced the dreadful sentence, that he should be pressed to death. The sentence was accordingly executed upon him two days after in the public market-place of Kilkenny. As the weights were heaping on the wretched man, he earnestly supplicated to be hanged; but it was beyond the power of the sheriff to deviate from the mode of punishment prescribed in the sentence, even this was an indulgence which could no longer be granted to him.

Records exist which strongly suggest that the opposite case was also not unknown; that is to say, prisoners who were genuinely deaf and dumb, but who were suspected of faking it and were treated accordingly. In 1735, a man was pressed to death at Nottingham for refusing to plead. All the evidence indicates that he had, in fact, been mute since birth.

As mentioned above, the *Peine forte et Dure* was sometimes applied as a means of persuading a reluctant prisoner to plead, and on others as a means of punishing the person, by killing him or her in a particularly painful and distressing fashion. If the aim was execution, then the weights would be piled on quickly, and a piece of sharp wood or stone would be placed underneath the victim to hasten death. The person condemned to such a death wished only to get the thing over and done with as quickly as possible. In 1676, a soldier called Major Strangeways killed a lawyer called Fussell, who had seduced his sister. He refused to plead to the charge of murder, and managed to obtain permission for some of his friends to be present when he was pressed to death. When the stones and iron weights failed to kill him quickly, he begged his friends to help ease his death. They did this by adding their own weight to that already pressing him down; climbing on top of the stone and iron. Major Strangeways' ribs collapsed and he died at once.

Cases where the object was to elicit an answer from the prisoner, so that the trial could take place, could last a long time. Four years before Major Strangeways died, a man called Henry Jones underwent the *Peine forte et Dure*. After refusing to plead, he was stretched out and loaded with 'as much weight as he could bear and more.' He lasted for an incredible forty-eight hours before dying. Even this is nothing compared with a case from 1359. It is alleged that a woman called Cecilia Ridgeway survived for forty days, being eventually pardoned by Edward III. Readers must judge for themselves how likely they find this!

In Chapter 6 we met a young man called Nathaniel Hawes. He had been acquitted of capital theft, by virtue of the jury engaging in pious perjury; they reduced the value of the goods which he had stolen below the value of £2. Hawes was branded on the hand and freed. This narrow escape does not seem to have taught him anything, because he later became a highwayman. After he had been captured, he refused to plead to the charge and so was put to the *Peine forte et Dure*. The wretched young man tried to endure 250lbs of stone being heaped on top of him but it took only seven minutes to change his mind. He pleaded not guilty, offered no defence, and was hanged at Tyburn on 21 December 1721. He was just nineteen years old.

This terrible punishment was still being inflicted on people as the eighteenth century progressed. In 1731, John Weekes had over 400lbs piled on top of him before he died. The last known case of this punishment being used in Britain was in 1741. Some years later, in 1772, it was abolished. From that time onwards, refusing to plead was entered as a plea of 'guilty' to the offence. This was changed in 1827 to the present arrangement, whereby somebody refusing to plead is regarded as pleading 'not guilty'.

10

Unofficial Death Sentences: Flogging and the Pillory

We have looked at various methods of execution – all of them, of course, designed to bring about the death of the condemned person. In one case, that of the *Peine forte et Dure*, death was a side effect. It is now time to look at two punishments awarded by the courts in the past, which sometimes amounted to *de facto* execution. The first of these was the pillory.

There is frequently some confusion between the pillory and the stocks. Although similar in purpose, the stocks and pillory differ in one vital aspect. In the stocks, the person undergoing the punishment would sit with his feet secured in a wooden frame. The idea was that he would be the object of ridicule, which could take the form of verbal abuse, mockery and even objects being thrown; typically rotten fruit, lumps of earth and even worse, excrement. In the pillory, the victim was standing and both his head and his hands were held in the frame, but they would be subjected to the same treatment meted out in the stocks. This apparently minor variation could make the difference between life and death. In the stocks, the victims could shield their heads with their arms; in the pillory the head and face were exposed to whatever was thrown. Usually, the worst that might be hurled would be clods of animal dung, or even the occasional dead cat. Sometimes though, if the offence for which the person was being pilloried excited particular disgust, stones and even bricks were thrown. Under such circumstances, being pilloried could amount to a sentence of stoning to death.

This is, of course, a very ancient tradition; allowing the community to inflict punishment upon a transgressor. The Bible prescribes stoning for certain offences, and the practice is still used for some sexual offences in modern-day Iran. It is entirely possible that the custom of pillorying grew out of this punishment, and was intended to be a modified and gentler way for society to express its disapproval.

Elizabeth Needham, popularly known as Mother Needham, ran an exclusive brothel in the St James' district of London. Unlike many eighteenth-century brothel keepers, Mother Needham specialised in young, virginal girls, rather than experienced prostitutes. She achieved this by meeting the wagons and coaches arriving in London from the countryside, and selecting the prettiest girls. She did not reveal the nature of her profession to them immediately and managed to ensnare quite a few innocent girls. Elizabeth Needham attained immortality as the most famous brothel keeper of her day. Hogarth used her as the model for Moll Hackabout in his series of engravings 'The Harlot's Progress', even Alexander Pope mentioned her in his satire *The Dunciad*.

For some years, Mother Needham's brothel was run more or less openly, having among its clientele many distinguished members of the aristocracy, and also high-ranking army officers. It was generally assumed that it was the patronage of such men which prevented the authorities from acting against Needham's establishment. Eventually though, there was an attempt to clean up London a little and raids were made on a number of brothels, Mother Needham's among them. She was arrested and on 29 April 1731, she was convicted of keeping a disorderly house; she was fined 1s and was ordered to stand twice in the pillory.

The crowds who gathered around the pillory in Park Place were in an extremely ugly mood. The seduction of young girls was viewed as a disgusting offence and the decision was taken not to insist that Needham stand in the pillory, but that she should be allowed to lay face down in front of it. It did her no good. She was pelted with bricks and rocks and taken back to the prison in an appalling state. She was due to be pilloried again on 4 May and expressed her terror at the prospect. She need not have worried though. So grave were her injuries that she died on 3 May.

Deaths like Mother Needham's were not a frequent occurrence, but neither were they especially rare. Sometimes, the crowd behaved very differently. When Daniel Defoe, the celebrated author of *Robinson Crusoe*, was pilloried in 1703 for annoying the authorities with his satirical writings, the crowd threw flowers to show their approval of him.

The year after Elizabeth Needham's death by stoning, there was another fatality. A man called John Waller had hit upon a marvellous money-making scheme. The authorities in different counties offered rewards for information leading to the conviction of thieves and highwaymen. Waller would accuse complete strangers of these offences, and with others would give evidence that they had attempted to commit robbery or theft. Once the innocent person was convicted and hanged, Waller and his gang would collect the reward. It was a truly hideous way of making a living, depending for its success upon the deaths of completely innocent people.

All good things come to an end and Waller was caught out after becoming a little too greedy. He was fined and sent to prison for perjury, but before this, he was to spend an hour in the pillory at Seven Dials, a very rough part of London at that time. On 13 June 1732, he was taken to the pillory. The sentence was that he should stand there for an hour, but he did not last this long. So horrible was the offence of which he had been found guilty, that a large crowd were waiting. He was stoned to death within minutes. At the subsequent inquest, the jury brought in a verdict of 'wilful murder by persons unknown'.

In 1753, a group of men in London hit upon an even more ingenious racket than that of John Waller. This plot entailed the use of a horse belonging to one of them. They persuaded a poor man called Tyler that they had no further use for the horse, and made a gift of it to him. Shortly afterwards, another member of the gang seized Tyler and the horse, and claimed that it was his horse and that Tyler had stolen it. Tyler was arrested, tried for horse theft and hanged. The gang picked up the reward and split it between themselves. They pulled the same stunt several more times before the authorities became suspicious. All four were sent to prison for seven years, but not before standing in the pillory. The *Newgate Chronicle* takes up the story:

> March the 5th, 1756, M'Daniel and Berry were set on the pillory at the end of Hatton Garden, and were so severely treated by the populace that their lives were supposed to be in danger.
>
> Egan and Salmon were taken to Smithfield on Monday the eighth of the same month, amidst a surprising concourse of people, who no sooner saw the offenders exposed on the pillory, then they pelted them with stones, brick-bats, potatoes, dead dogs and cats, and other things. The constables now interposed; but being soon overpowered, the offenders were left wholly to the mercy of an enraged mob. The blows they received occasioned their heads to swell to an enormous size; and they were nearly strangled by people hanging to the skirts of their clothes. They had been on the pillory about half an hour, when a stone striking Egan on the head, he immediately expired.

Deaths in the pillory continued throughout the eighteenth century. This punishment was, however, becoming increasingly rare, and in 1816 it was abolished for all offences other than perjury. Twenty years later, in 1837, it was done away with entirely.

The pillory was one punishment which could result in the death of the condemned. There was another. Titus Oates was a seventeenth-century crank who had a bee in his bonnet about Catholics. He claimed that they were planning to assassinate Charles II and to take over Britain. He managed to get the backing and support of some important people in the government, who had their own reasons for being militantly anti-Catholic. The whole thing was very similar to the communist hunt of the McCarthy era in America. A number of Jesuits were executed before common sense prevailed.

When King Charles died, and his brother ascended to the throne, things took a turn for the worse as far as Titus Oates was concerned. James II was himself a Catholic, and he soon saw to it that Oates was arrested and charged with perjury. He appeared before the notorious Judge Jeffreys in May 1685, and was convicted. The sentence was that he should stand in the pillory and then be whipped at the cart's tail from Aldgate to Newgate, and then two days later be whipped from Newgate to Tyburn. After this, he was to be imprisoned for life.

Oates had a rough time in the pillory, but the real ordeal which he faced was the whipping. It was widely assumed that this severe punishment was intended to kill him. Nobody could remember such a sentence ever having been passed. Whipping at the cart's tail was a common enough punishment, but not for such a distance as this.

On the day of the first whipping, Oates was stripped to the waist and his wrists were lashed together. A rope secured his bound wrists to the back of a cart, which moved off from Aldgate. It was clear from the start that the hangman had received special instructions to flog Oates with particular severity. At first he remained silent, but as the whipping continued and the blood ran down his back, he began to cry out in agony. According to a witness, 'his bellowings were frightful to hear.' By the time that Newgate was reached, he could no longer stand.

Since the next flogging was scheduled to take place just forty-eight hours later, and considering the pitiful state that he was in, a number of people made representations to the King, asking that he remit the second part of the flogging. James' reply was succinct, and indicated, perhaps, what he saw as the desired outcome of the exercise. 'He shall go through it if he has breath in his body,' he told those who begged for mercy on behalf of the seriously ill man lying in Newgate. On the morning of the second stage of his whipping, Titus Oates could not even stand, let alone walk. He was tied to a sledge and dragged from Newgate to Tyburn, the hangman whipping him throughout the journey. A man who later tended his wounds counted no fewer than 1,700 stripes – surely a record.

Incredibly, Oates survived and later recovered from this treatment. Others though, upon whom such corporal punishment had been inflicted, were not been so lucky. Flogging with the cat o'nine tails, for example, claimed a number of lives. Most of these were as a result of military punishment. As late as 1846, a soldier was flogged to death for a breach of military discipline. Private Frederick White died at Hounslow Barracks in July of that year. The problem with floggings in the British Army (up to the nineteenth century when the practice was abolished) was the sheer number of strokes awarded. During the Napoleonic Wars, the maximum number of strokes which could be inflicted was an astounding 1,200. This was actually carried out on half a dozen occasions. Floggings of this sort could cripple or even kill a man.

Sometimes a senior officer would order a flogging of such a nature, and it was obviously intended that the recipient would be killed by it. Sometimes, this would be overlooked by those in authority; from time to time, the person responsible would be called to account. This happened in the case of Governor Wall.

In 1779, Captain Joseph Wall, a career officer, was appointed governor of the island of Gorée, which is off the coast of Senegal. He had a garrison of British soldiers at his command. Governor Wall was not a popular man, being regarded by many as an inflexible martinet. He remained in post for three years, by the end of which time he was heartily detested by all those under his command. In 1782, shortly before he was due to retire and return to England, a group of soldiers petitioned him about various grievances. Wall chose to see this action as tantamount to mutiny. He was due to sail to England the next day, but postponed his departure so that he could show his men who was in charge. He had the man whom he regarded as the ringleader arrested, and held him in prison. This man was Sergeant Benjamin Armstrong. The next morning, Governor Wall announced that he would show these 'mutinous rascals' what it meant to cross a man like him. One minor detail which he overlooked was the formality of a court-martial, and this hastiness on the governor's part was to come back to haunt him.

Five slaves were ordered to tie Armstrong to a gun carriage and flog him. The governor declared that he should receive 800 lashes. These were to be given not with the cat o'nine tails, the standard instrument for flogging in the army at that time, but with ropes half an inch thick. The slaves were ordered to administer the beating and each man gave twenty-five lashes in turn, before making way for a fresh hand. They flogged the unfortunate Armstrong with special ferocity, largely because Wall was watching and threatening that if they did not, then he would have them flogged as well. Witnesses at his trial said that he was beside himself with rage, shouting at the slaves, 'Lay on you black beasts or I'll lay it on you. Cut him to the heart, cut his liver out.'

The whole affair was contrary not only to common humanity, but also to military law, because there had been no court-martial. Five days later, after Wall had sailed for England, Armstrong died of the wounds which he had received.

Shortly after he landed back in England, Governor Wall was arrested, news having been sent of the events in Africa. He managed to flee to the continent, where he stayed for the next eighteen years.

While living in exile in France, Joseph Wall married and this ultimately proved his downfall. He made several secret visits to England, but in 1801 returned openly. His motive was financial. His wife had a number of properties in the hands of trustees and he could only gain control of these by clearing his name and living in England. He expected to be arrested, but was astounded to be convicted of murder and sentenced to death. He was sixty-five at this time.

His defence was that he had been putting down a mutiny and so, severe measures were justified. None of the other witnesses, however, agreed that a mutiny had been taking place at the time. Since no pardon or reprieve was forthcoming, the old man was hanged. He was evidently shocked and distressed at finding himself condemned to death, so long after the event. We have a vivid contemporary account of the last minutes of Wall's life. It is to be found in the *Newgate Calendar*.

The prisoner entered. He was death's counterfeit, tall, shrivelled, and pale; and his soul shot so piercingly through the port-holes of his head, that the first glance of him nearly terrified me. I said in my heart, putting my pencil in my pocket, 'God forbid that I should disturb thy last moments!' His hands were clasped, and he was truly penitent. After the yeoman had requested him to stand up, he 'pinioned him', as the Newgate phrase is, and tied the cord with so little feeling, that the governor, who had not given the wretch the accustomed fee, observed, 'You have tied me very tight,' upon which Dr Ford ordered him to slacken the cord, which he did, but not without muttering. 'Thank you, sir,' said the governor to the doctor, 'it is of little moment.' He then observed to the attendant, who had brought in an immense iron shovelful of coals to throw on the fire, 'Ay, in one hour that will be a blazing fire'; then, turning to the doctor, questioned him, 'Do tell me, sir: I am informed I shall go down with great force; is that so?' After the construction and action of the machine had been explained, the doctor questioned the governor as to what kind of men he had at Gorée. 'Sir,' he answered, 'they sent me the very riff-raff.' The poor soul then joined the doctor in prayer; and never did I witness more contrition at any condemned sermon than he then evinced.

There was great dislike for the governor, and the crowd outside Newgate Prison voiced their disapproval loudly when he appeared on the scaffold. The hangman bungled the execution, placing the knot on the right side, instead of the left. This meant that when it tightened, the noose ended up at the back of the neck, guaranteeing that death would be from strangulation and not a broken neck. As the *Newgate Calendar* relates:

> From the knot of the rope turning round to the back of the neck, and his legs not being pulled, at his particular request, he was suspended in convulsive agony for more than a quarter of an hour.

TWENTIETH CENTURY: THE DECLINE OF THE DEATH PENALTY IN BRITAIN

Capital punishment ended in Britain in the twentieth century, but this was not because there was any great desire on the part of the public for its abolition. It was rather that, just as in the eighteenth century it became apparent that burning at the stake was an anachronism, so too did it seem, to liberal and progressive thinkers that the practice of hanging men and women was somehow out of keeping with the modern world. This was not, of course, the view of ordinary people, nor of the police or judiciary. A referendum on capital punishment at any time in the twentieth century, even thirty years after its abolition, would certainly have found a majority in favour of its retention. It was only among thoughtful and intelligent people that a mood of revulsion for the whole business began to become prevalent. This mood was reflected in both the type of crimes for which the death penalty was applied, and the frequency with which it was used. As an example of this changing perspective, let us look for a moment at the execution of women.

Throughout the history of this country, women have been hanged as well as men. Not as many, because women are statistically less likely than men to be burglars or murderers. Nevertheless, they have still been subjected to the death penalty. By the eighteenth century, there was a good deal of uneasiness about executing women and both juries and judges would do their best to avoid this happening. In the twentieth century, this realisation, that there was something distasteful about the hanging of women, gathered pace and the consequence was that very few women were actually hanged from 1900 onwards. From the beginning of the century, until the abolition of hanging in 1964, there were periods of ten or twelve years at a time when no women were executed in this country. Only sixteen women in total were hanged during the twentieth century; which meant that around 90 per cent of those actually condemned to death were reprieved. In practice, the death penalty was only exacted upon women who had used poison, killed children, or had been guilty of a particularly dreadful murder.

This is very similar to the 'pious perjury' at which we looked in Chapter 6. In theory, death was the mandatory punishment for murder for the first fifty years of the twentieth century, and yet the vast majority of women convicted of this offence were not hanged. The police, judiciary and Home Office worked together to try and avoid executing women.

This same tendency, not to impose the death penalty, was visible also in the numbers of men hanged in the last century. In 1903, for instance, twenty-seven people were hanged in England and Wales. This number gradually shrank, until the early fifties, by which time only twelve or fifteen a year were being executed. The slump in the number of executions bore no relation to the actual murder rate. The 1957 Homicide Act further reduced the incidence of executions, by introducing a distinction between capital and non-capital murder. After the passage of this Act, only certain types of murder would bring an automatic death sentence. These were murder in the course or furtherance of theft, murder by shooting or causing an explosion, murder whilst resisting arrest or escaping from custody and the murder of a police or prison officer in the course of his duty. A second murder, on a separate occasion, would also mean a death sentence.

The Homicide Act was an attempt at compromise, following events in Parliament the previous year. The Commons had voted in 1948 to abolish the death penalty, only for the Lords to refuse to endorse the move. Precisely the same thing happened in 1956. On 16 February 1956, the Commons voted upon another Private Members Bill, introduced by Sidney Silverman. The vote was 293 in favour of abolition, with 262 against. When it was sent to the Lords in June 1956, they rejected the Bill by the huge margin of 238 to 95. This was such a flagrantly undemocratic outcome that the government tried to placate MPs by bringing in a new Homicide Act, whose sole aim was to reduce the number of executions.

There was widespread dissatisfaction with the 1957 Homicide Act. Poisoning, for example, always regarded as the most loathsome form of murder, did not bring an automatic death sentence. Nevertheless, the new Act dramatically reduced the number of executions in Britain. In 1961, seven people were hanged, in 1963 three and in 1964 only two. It can thus be seen that the death penalty was falling into disuse over the course of the twentieth century. Its abolition represented, therefore, the recognition of a *de facto* situation.

The technique of hanging had been more or less perfected in the late nineteenth century. Still, it was not infallible. Consider the case of Alfred Stratton. Alfred and his brother Albert were a pair of petty criminals in their late twenties. On 26 March 1905, the two brothers forced their way into the living quarters above a shop and beat to death the elderly man and woman who ran the shop. Thomas Farrow was seventy-one and his wife sixty-five. It was a shocking crime, but a controversial clue was soon discovered. The rifled cashbox, which had been the target of the thieves' attention, was found to have a greasy smudge upon it which, on closer examination, turned out to be a fingerprint.

The science of fingerprinting was in its infancy, Scotland Yard's Fingerprinting Bureau had only been set up in 1901. However, since the Strattons were already suspected of the murder of the Farrows, it was easy enough to bring them in and take their prints. The print on the cashbox belonged to Alfred Stratton and although a murder case had never been decided on such evidence before, the jury convicted.

Albert, the younger of the two brothers found religion in the condemned cell. When the brothers met for the last time on the scaffold, in a double execution, Albert asked his brother, 'Alfred, have you given your heart to God?' There was a pause before his brother replied hoarsely that he had. Then the drop fell.

It was obvious that Alfred had not been rendered unconscious at once. The rope was shaking and swaying from side to side, as he struggled for breath. The post-mortem results, announced at the inquest, were uncompromising; Alfred Stratton had died of asphyxiation; his neck had not been broken.

Double executions were still a regular occurrence in British prisons at this time. Two years before the Strattons had died; the last double execution of women had been carried out at Holloway Prison. Twenty-nine-year-old Amelia Sach and an older woman, fifty-four-year-old Annie Walters, ran a nursing home for unmarried mothers. The women would stay at the home in west London and, after giving birth, Sach and Walters would, for a further fee, undertake to find foster parents for the babies. They were, in fact, what was known as 'baby farmers'. Rather than finding good homes for the babies, they were simply smothered and the fees pocketed by the two unscrupulous women running the operation.

For some time, it had been suspected by the police that something of this sort had been going on in London, because a number of babies' bodies had been fished from the Thames or found callously abandoned on rubbish tips.

Annie Walters was arrested with a dead baby actually in her possession. She admitted to having administered a morphine-based drug to the child in order to quieten it, but claimed not to know that the baby was dead. When police raided Amelia Sach's home, they found over 300 items of baby clothing. It was clear that the two women were 'baby farming' on an industrial scale. At their trial, both women were found guilty of murder and their execution was set for 3 February 1903.

Sach was in a state of collapse on the morning of her execution and had to be half carried to the scaffold. Her partner was in more robust spirits, and when they were both standing noosed and hooded on the drop, called out, 'Goodbye, Sach'. Her friend, though, had fainted and was being supported by the assistant hangman.

In Chapter 8, we looked at the last triple hanging to take place in Britain. It was very nearly a quadruple execution, but since the fourth victim would have been a woman, it was decided that this would not be an acceptable proceeding. At one time, mixed sex executions were routine, but they were falling out of favour by the end of the nineteenth century. The last hanging of a man and woman together, side-by-side on the same scaffold, took place in 1903.

Emily Swann and her husband lived in the Yorkshire town of Wombwell. She was a plain, forty-two-year-old woman whose marriage was apparently quite sound. That was until the day that a thirty-year-old man moved into the house as a lodger. John Gallagher was a miner and he and Emily began a torrid love affair, of which her husband William became aware. He started knocking her about and John Gallagher moved out. He kept in touch with Emily though, and was visiting a neighbour of hers when she arrived with two black eyes. Gallagher was so furious that he charged round to see her husband. Emily Swann followed and the neighbours heard the sounds of a fierce struggle. They also heard Emily's voice crying clearly, 'Give it to him Johnny.' William Swann was beaten to death; when the police were called, they arrested Emily, as John Gallagher had, rather ungallantly, made himself scarce. It was to be two months before he was tracked down and in December 1903, the pair appeared before Mr Justice Darling at Leeds.

There was no getting round those fatal words, 'Give it to him Johnny', and Mr Justice Darling correctly explained to the jury that this was a case of common purpose, with two people engaged in an enterprise which ended in the death of a victim. The jury found them both guilty and their execution was arranged to take place at Armley Prison in Leeds on 29 December 1903. Emily Swann was desperately afraid of death, and kept herself sane with the hope of a reprieve. When the governor told her that it had been decided that no reprieve would be granted, she went to pieces.

On the morning of her execution, Emily was utterly distraught. She lay on the floor of the condemned cell moaning. Surprisingly, she perked up a little after being given a glass of brandy and managed to walk to the gallows unaided. The sight that she encountered there was a grim one indeed, enough to shake the toughest nerves. Her one-time lover already stood on the drop, the noose around his neck and the white hood over his face. As she was being positioned, Emily said to him, 'Good morning, John.' He started in surprise, before replying warmly, 'Good morning, love.' Just before the trapdoors fell, Emily said, 'Goodbye, God bless you'. Twenty years later, when another adulterous couple had been found guilty of the murder of the husband in the case, the wife and lover were executed simultaneously in different prisons.

We saw earlier in this chapter that Alfred Stratton had choked to death, rather than having his neck broken by the drop. A similar thing happened to Alfred Neal, who was hanged in the same year as the Stratton brothers. In this case too, the death was recorded at the post-mortem as being caused by asphyxiation, and not by fracture/dislocation of the vertebrae in the neck. This problem was a direct consequence of the Aberdare Report, which was published at the end of the previous century. There had been so much concern at the instances of inadvertent decapitation, that the Aberdare committee had decided that a reduction in the length of the drops being used was desirable. They erred on the side of caution, which inevitably meant that some victims would not receive a long enough drop to break their necks. The table of drops drawn up by the Aberdare committee was not always followed, for this very reason. Experienced executioners made their calculations based on their observations of the condemned person. Weight was not the only factor to take into account. An old man with weak neck muscles would need a shorter drop than a healthy young man of the same weight. Hanging was an art, rather than a science.

One of the difficulties which remained with the arrangements for hanging was the distance to the gallows from the condemned person's cell in some prisons. The long ride from Newgate to Tyburn had rightly been done away with, but to a prisoner half-dead with fear, even a short walk through a corridor to the execution shed was more than could be expected. The solution to this problem was simple and logical, albeit a little grotesque. By the time that hanging came to be abolished, the gallows and the condemned cell were often part of one large room, separated only by a wooden dividing wall. For the weeks or months that they lay under sentence of death, the condemned prisoners were unknowingly living in the death chamber itself. Here is how the arrangement worked.

After the end of the First World War, there was a move to reduce the number of 'hanging prisons'. In those which remained, Wandsworth Prison in south London, for instance, 'execution suites' were built. These were constructed on three floors of a wing of a prison, using existing cells and landings. On one level would be the condemned cell and next to it the gallows chamber itself, which would take up an entire landing. The landing above this would accommodate the beam of the gallows, and the one directly beneath the gallows served as the pit into which the victim would fall when the trapdoors opened.

This system was better for all concerned. For one thing, it made the whole process of execution far quicker, which was more humane for the victim. From the moment that the door opened to admit the hangman, until the drop fell and the condemned person's neck broke, could take as little as ten seconds. The moveable wall was drawn back while the hangman was securing the wrists behind the back, and in the general confusion, the person would have had no time to realise what was happening. Most would be expecting to be led out of the cell to an execution shed; instead, they took a few short paces across the room to the waiting noose. From the point of view of the executioner, this was also a far better arrangement than having to drag a fainting man or woman up or down stairs and along corridors. Albert Pierrepoint had a party piece which he demonstrated to those assisting him during an execution. Before leaving the room to hang a man, he would sometimes light a cigar and then leave it burning in an ashtray. When he returned to the room after the hanging, he would draw on the cigar and show that it was still alight. Hanging people in twentieth-century Britain was that quick.

During the First World War, there was a sudden spate of executions for crimes other than murder. Since the 1840s, every execution undertaken in Britain had, with one exception, been for murder. The single case of an execution for a crime other than murder, was a man hanged in Chester in 1861, for a particularly terrible case of attempted murder. With the outbreak of war in 1914, the British began to round up German spies. Those who were caught were tried under the provisions of the Defence of the Realm Act, and if convicted were executed by firing squad. Eleven spies were shot at the Tower of London between 1914 and 1916. The execution of spies in the First World War was precisely the opposite of those in the Second World War. During the First World War, all spies, except for one, were shot. In the Second World War, all except one were hanged. The only spy hanged during the First World War was a German-American called Robert Rosenthal, who was executed at Wandsworth Prison on 15 July 1915.

During both world wars, there were unusual developments in capital punishment in this country. Things happen during wars which might not take place during peacetime. We saw above that nobody had been executed for any offence other than murder for many years, until the shooting of the German spies in the Tower between 1914 and 1916. Something which will almost certainly come as a surprise to readers is that in Britain, until as recently as 1945, men found guilty of rape, even when the victim was not killed, were executed. The circumstances which gave rise to this could only have happened in wartime.

Under the provisions of the United States (Visiting Forces) Act 1942, the American army was given the right to conduct capital trials on their own soldiers stationed here. This created a delicate situation for two different reasons. First, some offences which incurred the death penalty under American law, such as rape, were not capital offences in this country. This could and did mean that men were being executed for offences which, had they been committed in *this* country, would have brought the offender nothing worse than a prison sentence.

The second problem which arose was that the Americans had never abandoned the standard drop or 'short drop' method of hanging. This, combined with the use of the 'cowboy coil' style noose, meant American executioners were liable to strangle their victims, rather than break their necks cleanly, as we were doing to our own criminals. A compromise was eventually worked out.

The American forces were given a British prison for their own use. This was Shepton Mallet in Somerset, which is incidentally the oldest operating prison in the United Kingdom. The Americans took over the entire prison, even building their own gallows there. The British were happy to oblige with all this, but with one proviso. Any hangings were to be carried out by British, rather than American, executioners. Both sides were satisfied with this arrangement and between 1942 and 1945, a total of eighteen executions took place at Shepton Mallet. Two of these were by firing squad and the rest were hangings. Sixteen murderers and two rapists were executed, almost all by Thomas Pierrepoint and his nephew, Albert.

It seems strange to reflect that British executioners were, within living memory, at work in this country hanging men who had been convicted of a crime which had stopped being a capital offence 100 years before. Albert Pierrepoint later remarked upon what he found most shocking about these executions. As we have seen, hangings in this country were conducted very swiftly indeed, with the condemned person hardly aware of what was happening before they were falling through the trapdoor. American military executions were a very different matter. The prisoner was pinioned and taken onto the scaffold, as in the British method. There the similarity ended. In a British hanging, at this point the hood would be pulled down over the face, the noose placed round the neck of the condemned man and the trapdoors released. In American hangings, at this point there was a halt in the proceedings for five or six minutes while the charge was read out to the prisoner, the sentence was explained and the man was given an opportunity to make a final statement. The strain of this final delay must have been almost unbearable for a man about to be hanged and Albert Pierrepoint described this drawn-out process as 'sickening'.

In the early years of the twentieth century, there were still occasional cases of hangings which failed to break the neck. By the thirties, the technique had been perfected so that this never happened. Of thirty-eight prisoners hanged at Pentonville Prison between 1931 and 1950, the post-mortems showed that the neck was broken in every single case and there was no suggestion of asphyxiation.

In the twentieth century, hangmen and their assistants were no longer paid a wage, but the money they received for executions was still considerable by the standards of the day – a single hanging might pay the equivalent of a working man's wage for a week and a half. For this reason, there were strict rules about executioners touting for work by writing to prisons offering their services. These rules were drawn up in the early part of the century and applied until abolition in 1964. Every man was made aware of these rules when first he qualified as an assistant executioner. This followed a training course at a prison. Some of the rules were first instituted by the Aberdare Committee back in 1888:

1. Every person acting as assistant executioner is required to conform to any instructions he might receive from or on behalf of the High Sheriff as to the day and hour and route for going to and leaving the place of execution.

2. He is required to report himself at the prison at which an execution is to take place, and for which he has been engaged, not later than 4 o'clock on the afternoon preceding the day of execution.

3. He is required to remain in the prison from the time of his arrival until the completion of the execution, and until permission is given for him to live.

4. During the time he is in the prison he will be provided with lodging and board.

5. He should clearly understand that his conduct and general behaviour should be respectable, not only at the place and time of the execution, but before and subsequently, that he should avoid attracting public attention in going to or from the prison, and he is prohibited from giving to any person particulars on the subject of his duties for publication.

There then followed the rates of pay for helping at an execution, and a warning that records would be kept of the behaviour of those taking part in executions. Rule 8 went on to specify that:

It will be considered objectionable conduct for any person to make an application to a sheriff or under-sheriff for employment in connection with an execution, and such conduct may involve removal of such person's name from the list.

Four years after the end of the Second World War, a Royal Commission was set up to consider whether the circumstances under which capital punishment for murder was applied should be changed. Many witnesses were summoned to give evidence to the commission, including the Lord Chief Justice and the Archbishop of Canterbury. The actual terms of reference for the commission were as follows:

To report and consider whether liability under the criminal law in Great Britain to suffer capital punishment should be limited or modified, and if so, to what extent and by what means, for how long, and under what conditions persons who would otherwise be liable to capital punishment should be detained, and what changes in the existing law and the prison system would be required; and to inquire into and take account of the position in those countries whose experience and practice might throw light upon these questions.

The Home Office submitted a memorandum to the Royal Commission which gave some details of the days leading up to the execution. It is worth quoting in full, as it gives a fascinating insight into the mundane details of capital punishment as practiced in the mid-twentieth century:

Immediately a prisoner sentenced to death returns from court, he is placed in a cell for condemned prisoners and is watched night and day by two officers. Amenities such as cards, chess, dominoes etc., are provided in the cell and the officers are encouraged to – and in fact invariably do – join the prisoner in these games.

Newspapers and books are also provided. Food is supplied from the main prison kitchen, the prisoner being placed on hospital diet, with such additions as the medical officer considers advisable. A pint of beer or stout is supplied on daily request and ten cigarettes or half an ounce of pipe tobacco are allowed unless there are medical reasons to the contrary. The prisoner may smoke in his cell as well as at exercise.

It is the practice for the governor, medical officer and chief officer to visit a prisoner under sentence of death twice daily, and the chaplain or minister of any other denomination has free access to him.

He may be visited by such of his relations, friends and legal advisors as he desires to see and as are authorised to visit him and he is given special facilities to write and receive letters.

This account is chilling in its matter-of-fact discussion of the day-to-day trivia of the last days of a human being. Cards and dominoes, newspapers, a pint of beer and ten cigarettes a day; it sounds like a dreary boarding house rather than the prelude to a violent death! The same Home Office memorandum describes the process of execution itself, making it sound as unremarkable as a visit by a man from the council to look at the drains:

On the morning of the execution it is usual for the chaplain to spend the last hour with the prisoner and remain with him until the execution is over.

Some twenty minutes before the time fixed for the execution the High Sheriff, or more usually the Under Sheriff, arrives at the prison, and a few minutes before it is due, proceeds with the governor and medical officer to the place of execution.

The executioner and his assistant wait outside the condemned cell, with the chief officer and officer detailed to conduct the prisoner to the execution chamber. On a signal given by the Sheriff they enter and the executioner pinions the prisoner's arms behind his back. He is escorted to the drop with one officer on either side. The Sheriff, the Governor and the medical officer enter the execution chamber by another door.

The prisoner is placed on the drop on a marked spot so that his feet are directly across the division of the trap doors. The executioner places a white cap over the prisoner's head and places the noose round his neck, while the assistant pinions his legs. When the executioner sees that all is ready he pulls the lever.

As recounted by the Home Office, hanging a man is about as dull and routine an affair as one can imagine. The reality was sometimes a little different. Take the case of Karl Richard Richter.

Karl Richter was born in the Sudetenland on 29 January 1912. On the night of 31 May 1941, he parachuted into this country, landing near the village of London Colney in Hertfordshire. On landing, he buried his parachute and changed into civilian clothing – by doing so, he automatically became a spy rather than an enemy soldier. His career in espionage lasted only thirty minutes from the time he left his landing spot. A lorry driver asked him for directions and Richter was uncommunicative. A short distance down the road, the driver of the lorry stopped a policeman to ask for directions, mentioning the surly individual he had just met. It was enough to rouse the police officer's curiosity and he cycled off to try and find the man. Richter was thus arrested before he had a chance to do anything at all.

He was offered the opportunity to double-cross his masters in Germany and become, in effect, an agent for the British; an offer which he contemptuously refused. His trial, under the Treachery Act, was held *in camera* at the Old Bailey between the 21st and 24th of October. He was found guilty and sentenced to death. His appeal was dismissed the following month, and his execution was scheduled to be held at Wandsworth Prison on 10 December.

When he arrived at the prison, on the day before the execution, Albert Pierrepoint observed Richter in the exercise yard. The German spy was 6ft 2in tall and weighed over 15 stone. He was not a fat man; it was all muscle. At eight o'clock the following morning, Pierrepoint and the officials entered the condemned cell, and it was then that the hangman realised that things were not going to go smoothly. It was customary for the condemned man to sit with his back to the door on the morning of his execution. This meant that the executioner could be across the room in a few strides, tap the man on the shoulder and, as he rose, move his arms behind his back to fasten the wrists together with a thin leather strap. On this occasion, Richter was standing facing the door and, when it opened, he made a sudden dive. He was not aiming to escape though; he leapt headfirst at the stone wall. It was later thought that he may have been trying to knock himself out, so that he would be unconscious when he was hanged.

In the event, he only stunned himself and as the executioner, his assistant and the prison officers moved towards him, he jumped up and began fighting for his life. It was a desperate struggle. Trouble had been expected and two more guards were waiting in the corridor. They now rushed in and tried to subdue Richter, to enable the execution to take place. Eventually, with two men sitting on his legs and the others gripping an arm each, it was possible to bring his arms behind his back so that Pierrepoint could fasten his wrists together. As he turned to lead the way into the execution chamber, there was a cry of alarm from behind him. So strong was the German that he had managed to burst the buckle of the strap, and his hands were now free. The fight started again. After more struggling, the strap was once more fastened and the condemned man was dragged to the scaffold. He fought ferociously every inch of the way.

At last, with Richter on the drop, Pierrepoint's assistant, a man called Steve Wade, was able to get the strap around his ankles. He then dived off the trap-doors. At that moment, the most horrifying incident of all occurred.

The purpose of the white hood was to prevent the condemned person from seeing when the trap was about to be sprung. In the past, some men had been known to try to leap off at the last moment. Such an incident occurred in 1924.

Patrick Mahon was convicted of a particularly gruesome murder. He had killed his pregnant mistress and dismembered the body, trying to dispose of it by boiling parts of it in saucepans. Mahon was in a pitiful state when brought to the condemned cell after his trial, crying and moaning and having to be carried bodily. He recovered somewhat while waiting to be hanged, although he lost 9lbs in weight, hardly eating after he was sentenced to death. Once he had been placed on the scaffold, and noosed and hooded, he guessed instinctively when the trapdoors were about to open and jumped at the last moment, presumably hoping to land on the edge of the scaffold. He misjudged the distance though and banged his back as he fell. His neck was found to be broken in two places at the post-mortem, rather than the usual single fracture dislocation. It was this fear which had also led to the pinioning of the legs on the scaffold.

Returning to Karl Richter's execution, just as Pierrepoint was pulling the lever to operate the drop, Richter suddenly jumped, at precisely the moment that the trapdoors opened. To his horror, the executioner saw that the noose had opened and was seemingly about to slip over Richter's head. By sheer chance, the rope actually caught on his nose and tightened as usual. Incredibly, his neck was broken as neatly as in any other hanging.

Writing about this execution in his diary, the assistant executioner said that it had taken seventeen minutes from entering the cell until the condemned man was hanging on the end of the rope.

This was admittedly an extreme case, but there were quite a few instances of prisoners fainting at the last moment and having to be dragged semi-conscious to the gallows. The Home Office was very keen that what happened at executions should remain secret. Following the abolition of public hanging in 1868, it had become the custom to allow newspaper reporters to witness executions. This was not entirely satisfactory, because if a man had his head torn off, rather than dying instantly, or was choked to death convulsively on the end of the rope, the public learned all the gory details. Increasingly, as the twentieth century drew on, hangings were conducted with no reporters present and only official witnesses such as prison staff and the chaplain. The last hanging at which a journalist was present took place in 1934, but this was a rare exception.

None of this stopped the rumours reaching the ears of those outside the prison. Edith Thompson's hanging, in 1923, is a case in point. Although it was denied at the time, it later emerged that the condemned woman, a suburban housewife hanged for her adultery as much as anything else, had not walked cheerfully to her death, despite the Home Office evidence to the Royal Commission suggesting that prisoners generally did. Buoyed by hope of a reprieve, almost until the last minute, Edith Thompson went mad with terror when the truth struck home that she was really going to hang. Those waiting outside the cell on the morning of her execution could hear her moaning and wailing, and she was quite unable to walk to the scaffold or even stand upright after she had been carried there by two men. She was in a dead faint when she went through the trapdoors. A final and exceedingly gruesome aspect of this execution is that for reasons which are unclear, Edith Thompson was haemorrhaging heavily, with blood running down her legs. The man who had carried out this execution, John Ellis, never recovered from the events of that morning and later killed himself by cutting his own throat with an open razor.

All those who participated in executions knew that their jobs depended upon remaining silent about anything they saw. This naturally included the executioners themselves. Later, hangmen were required to sign the Official Secrets Act. Staff at the prison knew that they might be subject to disciplinary proceedings if they discussed what they saw during an execution, and so had a strong motive not to gossip or write about their experiences. Governments were especially anxious that nothing should appear in the newspapers giving any sort of details about what went on at hangings.

The problem arose after the retirement of a hangman. Such was the public appetite for details about executions, that a retired or sacked hangman could always be sure of selling his story to the newspapers. James Berry, the hangman whose services had been dispensed with after accidentally decapitating one too many of his victims, went one better than a series of newspaper articles. He had a series of 'magic lantern' slides made and devised a stage show; touring northern theatres and music halls with his anecdotes about hanging. Attempts were made to put a stop to these exhibitions on the grounds of public decency, but they came to nothing.

Another former hangman who cashed in on his experiences was Henry Pierrepoint. He had been removed from the approved list of executioners in 1910, for turning up at an execution drunk and for fighting with the assistant hangman. After begging for his job back, he sold his reminiscences to the newspapers not once, but twice. It is an indication of the voracious interest of the general public for details of hangings that, after reading his memoirs in 1916, newspaper readers were still eagerly devouring identical revelations from Pierrepoint in *Reynolds News* in 1922.

There was not a great deal that the government could do about Henry Pierrepoint selling his story to the Sunday papers. He had been a hangman before the passage of the Official Secrets Act. It was a different matter with his son though, who, when he first became an assistant executioner in 1932, had signed the Official Secrets Act. In doing so, he agreed not to divulge anything which he did or saw in the course of his work for the government. He was placed in precisely the same position as a civil servant entrusted with sensitive information.

In early 1956, Albert Pierrepoint, the most prolific hangman in British history, resigned. His resignation was ostensibly prompted by a dispute over a payment for his time in the case of an execution in Manchester, which was cancelled after a reprieve. The full details of this affair are to be found in Chapter 13. There was considerably more to the matter than met the eye though, and the full details did not emerge until many years later. While arguing over pay, Pierrepoint did not reveal to the Prison Commissioners that after tendering his resignation, he had entered into a contract with the *Empire News and Sunday Chronicle* to serialise his experiences as hangman. He was to be paid a sum equivalent in today's terms to around £500,000.

A week after Albert Pierrepoint had written to the Home Office asking to be removed from the approved list of executioners, they wrote back asking if there was any truth in the rumours that he was planning to sell his memoirs to a Sunday newspaper. He was reminded of the confidentiality agreement which he had signed in 1932, and also of the provisions of the Official Secrets Act. He replied, telling them that he was planning to disclose nothing which was not already in the public domain.

The first article appeared on Sunday 18 March, so swiftly after his resignation that it was obvious that he had already been negotiating with the newspaper before he had asked for his name to be taken off the list. There was nothing particularly objectionable about the piece, except that it promised in the following weeks to give details of the last moments of some of the most notorious men and women Pierrepoint had hanged. This alarmed the Home Office and a few days later a detective superintendent visited both the publishers of the newspaper and also Pierrepoint himself. It did no good.

The next instalment was a detailed account of Reginald Christie's last moments. It was at this point that the Home Office took the gloves off and told the publishers that if there were any future revelations of the sort, an action would be brought against them under the Official Secrets Act. This had the effect of ending the series of articles. It is not known if Pierrepoint had to return the fee which he had been paid.

It is interesting to compare the government's reaction to these anecdotes, at a time when hanging was still being carried out, with how they handled the release of a book of his more detailed memoirs in 1973, ten years after the end of hanging. Although these too, technically, breached the Official Secrets Act, nobody bothered to menace either Albert Pierrepoint or the publishers this time. It was old news.

We end this chapter with examples of two very different reactions to the prospect of being hanged. One might suppose that anybody facing the experience of being executed would recoil in abject terror, but this was not generally what happened. The majority of condemned people found the courage to walk to their deaths with dignity. Indeed, some of those who were hanged seemed almost to welcome the event as an end to their suffering. The two cases at which we will look are both of men who actually pleaded guilty to a capital charge, knowing that they would face the gallows as a result.

At his trial in April 1908, Thomas Bone pleaded guilty to the murder of his wife. He was sentenced to death and was due to be hanged in Ayr Prison on 20 May. Henry Pierrepoint and his assistant, John Ellis, arrived at the prison at the same moment as a King's Messenger carrying a reprieve. The governor of the prison asked Pierrepoint if he would like to accompany him to the condemned cell to give Bone the good news. The condemned man was sitting quietly, reading the Bible. When he was told that he would not hang the next day, the condemned man became extremely distressed, weeping and shouting that he wanted to be with his wife. The news of the reprieve was not at all to his liking. Four years later, while serving the sentence of life imprisonment to which his death sentence had been commuted, he hanged himself in his cell.

Thomas Bone's behaviour in the condemned cell contrasts starkly with that of another man who pleaded guilty to murder, in the expectation of being hanged. This was the extraordinary case of Frederick Arthur Cross, in 1955. Cross' wife left him, taking their two young children with her. He was so distraught that he bought some poison with the intention of taking his own life. However, he could not bring himself to swallow the poison, and so began one of the strangest suicides ever recorded. Cross decided to murder a random stranger so that he would be hanged. On 25 February, a travelling salesman knocked on his door, asking for directions. Cross offered to jump in his car and show him the way. He then stabbed twenty-eight-year-old Donald Lainton to death with a pair of scissors. After committing this pointless murder, Cross gave himself up to the police, insisting that he did not wish to defend himself; he simply wished to hang.

On 5 July, he pleaded guilty to murder at the Birmingham Assizes and was duly sentenced to death. The next day, he woke up in the condemned cell and suddenly realised that perhaps he did not wish to die after all. There followed a flurry of activity as he appealed against the sentence and his wife lobbied for a reprieve. It was to no avail.

On the morning of Wednesday 27 July, Albert Pierrepoint and Harry Allen entered the condemned cell at Winson Green Gaol. Cross went mad with panic, refusing to allow his wrists to be secured behind his back. It took help from the warders before he could be pinioned and he fought all the way to the scaffold, screaming in terror. Getting him onto the drop was a slow business and he resisted all efforts to strap his ankles together. It was one of the most distressing executions ever witnessed at the prison.

THE END OF CAPITAL PUNISHMENT IN BRITAIN

John Allen West, a fifty-three-year-old laundry-van driver lived alone in the northern town of Workington. On the evening of 6 April 1964, he arrived home from work as usual. In the early hours of the following morning, his neighbours heard a noise from West's house. They looked out of the window and saw a car driving off. Uneasy, they called the police, who found the van driver lying dead in his home. He had been beaten and stabbed. It was not a difficult crime to solve. A raincoat was found which did not belong to the dead man. In the pocket was a medallion inscribed 'G.O. Evans, July 1961' and a piece of paper bearing a name and address in Liverpool. The name was that of Norma O'Brian, a seventeen-year-old factory worker. She identified the medallion and told the police that she had seen it being worn by 'Ginger' Owen Evans, a man whom she had met while staying with her sister in Preston.

Twenty-four-year-old Owen Evans was lodging with Peter Allan and his wife. Both men worked at the same dairy together, and both had criminal records. Evans had in his possession a watch belonging to John West, which made this a capital crime under the 1957 Homicide Act – being murder in the furtherance of theft. Both men admitted to having been in the murdered man's house on the night he died, although each blamed the other for his murder. In court, they both attempted what are known as 'cut-throat' defences, in which each man tried to put the full blame on the other. As is usual in such cases, the jury found there was nothing to choose between them and both were convicted of capital murder at Manchester Crown Court in July 1964. They were sentenced to death.

Twenty-one-year-old Peter Allan went berserk when he learned that no reprieve was to be forthcoming. During the final visit by his wife and two children, he flung himself at the screen separating him from his family, breaking his wrist in the process. It was to no avail. At eight o'clock in the morning on 13 August 1964, he was hanged at Liverpool. At the same moment, Owen Evans was hanged in Manchester. These were the last executions to take place in Britain.

There have always been those who found the ritual of execution degrading, unenlightening and ultimately useless for the deterrence of crime. We saw in an earlier chapter that Charles Dickens had written to *The Times*, expressing his disgust at the behaviour of the crowds at an execution in London during the 1840s. Although Dickens' censure was directed at the public nature of such events, rather than the death penalty itself, a number of prominent people at the time were convinced that executions achieved nothing, and had no role at all in keeping down the murder rate.

Perhaps the keenest argument, demonstrating the futility and ultimate absurdity of the whole business, was that developed by some Victorian essayists. They pointed out that, if the aim of executions was deterrence, then it did not logically matter whether the man or woman being hanged was actually guilty of the crime. As long as people believed that the condemned person was guilty, this would still act as a deterrent! A system which could rely for its effectiveness upon the judicial death of innocent people had to be flawed in some way.

Particularly revolting executions often converted observers to the abolitionist viewpoint. The hanging of Robert Goodale at Norwich Castle, in 1885, was particularly distressing for witnesses. The condemned man struggled desperately to avoid being hanged and the affair culminated with the inadvertent removal of the victim's head. At that time, reporters were allowed to witness executions and as a consequence, newspapers were well-informed about the precise circumstances surrounding hangings. Following Goodale's hanging, a local newspaper, the *Eastern Daily Press*, carried a strong editorial denouncing not just Goodale's execution, but the practice of capital punishment itself. After describing the accidental decapitation of Goodale as 'a catastrophe unparalleled in the history of executions' the lead writer went on to say:

> We are persuaded that capital punishment is useless to prevent murders and that it is an offence to society. It shocks human nature. Every cultured sense revolts at the spectacle of a man legally done to death.

The fact is that the general public then, as indeed now, were overwhelmingly in favour of the execution of those found guilty, of some types of murder.

Although the death sentence was mandatory, there were many reprieves and those actually hanged were often those where the murder had some feature which exacerbated the offence; making it in some way unusual. Some types of murder almost never resulted in reprieves – child murders, the killing of police officers, poisoning and so on.

In the early twentieth century, those agitating for the complete abolition of the death penalty were widely viewed as cranks. They were typified by the eccentric Mrs Violet Van der Elst, who used to arrive outside prisons in her Rolls-Royce on the night before an execution. She then spent the next twelve hours singing hymns through a loudspeaker. Regarded by the authorities as a nuisance, and by ordinary people as a misguided crackpot, Mrs Van der Elst was thought to exemplify abolitionists; well meaning and idealistic, but hopelessly out of touch with the man and woman in the street.

The impetus towards abolition really picked up pace following the end of the Second World War. In 1948, the Labour MP Sidney Silverman introduced a Private Members Bill, calling for the suspension of the death penalty for a period of five years. This was promptly passed by the Commons, which at this time had, of course, a Labour majority. The Home Secretary, James Chuter-Ede, announced that he would reprieve all those sentenced to death until the outcome of Sidney Silverman's bill was known. There were accordingly no executions in the United Kingdom between March 1948, when the Bill was passed by the Commons, and October of the same year when it reached the Lords. They rejected it and executions began to take place once again. In the same year, a Royal Commission was set up, under Sir Ernest Gowers, to examine all aspects of the death penalty as it was operating in Britain.

It was to be five years before the Royal Commission published their report, and it contained few surprises. It did not advocate the abolition of the death penalty, nor even its restriction. It was explicitly stated that such a move should only take place if the great majority of the public were in favour of abolition; something which has never been the case in this country. Some concern was expressed about the mental health of those tried for murder, and closer examination for psychiatric abnormalities was recommended. Apart from that, it was suggested that two executioners, rather than just one working with two assistants, should be used at double executions in future. It was felt that having only one hangman for two men slowed down the process, and imposed unacceptable mental suffering upon those being hanged. In the event, there was to be only one more double execution in Britain before the practice ended. This took place less than a year after the publication of the Royal Commission's report.

Perhaps the most shocking part of the Royal Commission's report was hidden away in the small print. It was stated that the commission did not believe that the death penalty acted as a deterrent to murder. Since this had been the main justification for hanging people for years, it was a startling admission.

Other methods of execution were examined and found wanting. Some favoured shooting, but as the report observed tartly, 'it does not possess even the first requisite of an efficient method, the certainty of causing immediate death.' There was considerable unease about the mechanism of the reprieve system. Some 45 per cent of those sentenced to death were reprieved; in most cases the decisions were made, and the recommendations forwarded to the Home Secretary, by unelected civil servants.

As the fifties passed, several cases occurred which created unease. Not so much about the principle of capital punishment, most people were happy with that, but more about the way that it was being applied in specific circumstances. In 1952, for instance, two teenage tearaways, one aged nineteen and the other just sixteen, broke into a warehouse in south London. The younger boy was armed with a revolver and when the police came, they quickly seized the older of the two and arrested him. He called out to his friend for help, crying, 'Let him have it, Chris!' His companion in crime did indeed 'let him have it', shooting dead a police officer. At their trial, before Lord Chief Justice Goddard, it emerged that Derek Bentley, the older of the two youths, had learning difficulties and a mental age of eleven. He was, nevertheless, sentenced to death for the murder, on the grounds that he had incited the young man with the pistol to open fire. Sixteen-year-old Christopher Craig, being under eighteen, was sent to prison for life, he was released ten years later. Derek Bentley was hanged on 28 January 1953.

In an interview some years later, Lord Goddard claimed that he had assumed that Derek Bentley would be reprieved, and blamed the Home Secretary of the day for the boy's death. In 1993, Bentley was granted a Royal Pardon and five years later his conviction for murder was quashed. Had he been alive by that time, he would have been entitled to a retrial.

One of the things that many people found disturbing about Derek Bentley's execution was his age; he was, after all, only a teenager. Combined with the fact that he did not actually have a hand in the murder, it seemed a clear miscarriage of justice. Another miscarriage of justice had occurred several years earlier, but only came to light in 1953. In that year John Christie, a serial strangler of women, was tried and executed. During his trial, it emerged that his lodger, a feeble-minded Welsh man called Timothy Evans, had been hanged for strangling his wife and daughter in 1950. At Evans' trial, Christie gave evidence against him, but Evans insisted that it was Christie who had killed his family.

It was quite absurd to suppose that there could have been two multiple stranglers of women living in the same house, committing murders without the other's knowledge! Timothy Evans was awarded a posthumous pardon in 1966. At Christie's execution, he complained after being pinioned that his nose was itching. Albert Pierrepoint, the executioner, reassured him, saying, 'It won't bother you for long.'

During the 1950s, the hanging of women attracted unfavourable attention. Three women were hanged in that decade; Louise Merrifield in 1953, Styllou Cristofi in 1954 and Ruth Ellis in 1955. Ruth Ellis was a glamorous, twenty-eight-year-old blonde and her execution was the last to be carried out on a woman.

In 1955, Sidney Silverman once again introduced a Bill to abolish hanging. It was passed by the Commons in February 1956, and again the Home Secretary announced that there would be no executions until the will of Parliament was known. Predictably, the Lords threw out the Bill, but between August 1955 and July 1957 there were no executions in this country. It was perfectly clear by now that the House of Commons was determined to put an end to capital punishment.

In 1960 and 1961 two cases came to trial which showed perfectly, that hanging was no deterrent to murder. One of these cases was of the youngest person to be executed in Britain in the twentieth century. The Children's Act of 1908 specifically forbade the execution of anybody under the age of sixteen. Before that, it was theoretically possible for a child to hang. The last person of this age to be sentenced to death was in 1932, when sixteen-year-old Harold Wilkins was convicted of a sexually motivated murder at the Stafford Assizes. He was later reprieved. The following year, the Children and Young Persons Act raised the minimum age at which an individual could be executed to eighteen.

On the night of Saturday, 25 June 1960, twenty-three-year-old Alan Jee was set upon by four vicious young men, who were intent upon committing what we would now call a mugging. One of the gang punched Jee, knocking him to the ground, whereupon the others began a ferocious and sustained assault. The youngest of the group, eighteen-year-old Francis Forsyth, known to his friends as 'Flossie', kicked Alan Jee repeatedly in the head with his fashionable winkle-picker shoes. While he did so, the others went through the victim's pockets, looking for money. Jee suffered catastrophic brain damage during the robbery, and died two days later without regaining consciousness. He had become engaged shortly before the murder and his fiancée was at his side when he died.

Because the murder had been committed 'in the course or furtherance of theft', this made it a capital offence under the provisions of the recently passed 1957 Homicide Act. Four young men were arrested for the murder; Norman Harris and Christopher Darby, both aged twenty-three, Terrence Lutt, aged seventeen and eighteen-year-old Forsyth. At their trial later that year at the Old Bailey, all but Darby were found guilty of capital murder. Lutt, being only seventeen, was detained at Her Majesty's Pleasure, leaving Harris and Forsyth to face the death sentence. Despite his youth, there was little sympathy for Forsyth who, by all accounts, was a particularly nasty piece of work. Because double executions were no longer carried out, Harris and

Forsyth were hanged simultaneously on 10 November 1960 in different prisons; Harris in Pentonville and Forsyth in Wandsworth. Forsyth slept badly on the night before his execution and constantly cried out that he did not wish to die.

Despite the fact that hanging had been perfected by the fifties and sixties, with a precisely broken neck resulting from every execution; there were still mishaps and slip-ups. One of these occurred at Forsyth's hanging. It was the custom to ensure that the condemned man was sitting with his back to the door, so that when the executioner entered, he would not jump back in panic. We saw in the last chapter, during the execution of Karl Richter, what the ill effects of ignoring this convention could be. A similar thing happened when Francis Forsyth was about to be executed. When Harry Allen, the hangman, entered the room, he assumed as a matter of course that the man sitting with his back to the door was the one whom he had to hang. He entered the cell, strode swiftly to the chair and gripped the man by the arm, urging him to his feet. The person he had seized was not in fact Francis Forsyth but the Reverend Philips, the chaplain consoling the boy who was about to die. Fortunately, this confusion was quickly cleared up.

Another glitch in the smooth process of taking a man's life judicially, occurred at the execution of Derek Bentley in 1953. Albert Pierrepoint, the executioner who hanged Bentley, was proud of the speed with which he was able to deprive a man of his life. Typically, it took no more than ten or twelve seconds, although his personal best was an astonishing eight seconds from entering the cell until the man was hanging on the end of the rope. At Bentley's execution, Pierrepoint was a little too fast. When he pulled the release, one of the prison officers was not quite clear of the trap. He overbalanced when the trapdoors opened and actually fell into the pit. Luckily, he was not badly injured.

There was a curious and exceedingly revealing sequel to Francis Forsyth's execution. On the morning of the execution, a friend of Forsyth's was sitting in his car outside a branch of Lloyds Bank in the south-coast resort of Worthing. At nine o'clock this friend, twenty-year-old Victor Terry, heard on the car radio that Forsyth had been hanged. Less than an hour later, he shot dead sixty-one-year-old Henry Pull, a security guard, while attempting to rob the bank. This too was a capital crime, involving as it did both the use of a firearm and the furtherance of theft. He advanced the unusual defence that the crime was caused by his channelling the spirit of the American gangster 'Legs' Diamond. This was not enough to save him. On 26 May 1961, he was hanged on the same gallows that had claimed the life of his friend. A few seconds before eight o'clock on the morning of his execution, Terry lit a cigarette, which he was allowed to keep in his mouth during the pinioning and walk to the scaffold. Only as he was about to place the hood over the young man's head did executioner Harry Allen take the cigarette from his lips. When Henry Pierrepoint hanged William Foy in 1909, he chose not to deprive his victim of a last smoke, placing the hood over the man's head without removing his cigarette.

Nothing could more clearly illustrate the futility of relying upon capital punishment as a deterrent to crime, than the execution of Victor Terry. Here was a man who had been perfectly aware of the perils of murder, having been well-acquainted with another young man who had paid the ultimate price. It had not prevented him from following a precisely similar path, which led him to die on the same gallows as his friend.

Francis Forsyth was not quite the last teenager to be hanged in Britain. In April 1960, nineteen-year-old Anthony Miller and his sixteen-year-old friend James Denoven, were making money by beating and robbing homosexuals in Glasgow. They went too far one night, beating John Cremin so badly that he died of his injuries. Their haul from this robbery was £67; a considerable sum of money at that time. The two young men were tracked down and charged with capital murder. Being under eighteen, Denoven was sent to prison for life, but Anthony Miller was sentenced to death. The youngster was hanged at Barlinnie Prison in Glasgow, on 22 December 1960. He was the second to last person to be executed in Scotland.

Hanging was coming to an end, even without further legislation. The numbers of executions carried out in this country had been declining since the beginning of the twentieth century, from twenty-nine in England and Wales in 1902, to fifteen in 1951. A tiny number were carried out in other parts of the United Kingdom. There was an even more dramatic decline in executions with the passage of the Homicide Act in 1957. The year following Victor Terry's execution, only three hangings took place in the whole of the United Kingdom. One of these was seized upon by abolitionists and became something of a *cause célèbre*.

In August 1961, a man and woman sitting in a parked car were abducted by a gunman. He shot the man dead and then raped the woman, later shooting her too. She survived but was paralysed from the waist down. A twenty-four-year-old petty criminal called James Hanratty was arrested and charged with capital murder. His defence was one of alibi. He first claimed that he had been in Liverpool at the time of the murder and then, when that failed, suddenly decided that he had been in the Welsh seaside resort of Rhyl. Unsurprisingly, the jury were not impressed with this defence, he was found guilty and sentenced to death. He was hanged in Bedford Prison on 4 April 1962. Many people believed that a miscarriage of justice had occurred; and it was this sort of case, combined with others at which we have looked in this chapter, which persuaded the Labour Party to fight the 1964 General Election with a manifesto committed to the abolition of hanging for murder.

So pivotal was the Hanratty case to abolitionists that it did not fade away with the end of capital punishment in Britain. Instead, it was constantly cited, alongside that of Timothy Evans and Derek Bentley, as the sort of injustice which was bound to occur for as long as one executed people. Such errors were impossible to set right, claimed campaigners. Books were written about the case and it was mentioned countless times whenever conversation turned to the subject of wrongful execution. Despite the fact that two official enquiries, one in 1967 and the other in 1975, both found that there had been no miscarriage of justice, relatives of Hanratty continued to fight to clear his name. In 1997, the results of yet another enquiry led to the Hanratty case being referred by Home Secretary, Michael Howard, to the newly-formed Criminal Cases Review Commission. Ever since DNA testing had been devised in the 1980s, Hanratty's family had been urging that tests be carried out on the samples which still existed from the case.

In 2001, James Hanratty's body was exhumed and samples of DNA were obtained. These were compared with two samples from the original evidence. One of these was mucus from the handkerchief used to wrap the murder weapon, and the other was semen stains from the underwear of the woman who had been raped. Both proved without any doubt that Hanratty had committed the murder, and his appeal was dismissed.

When Harold Wilson became Prime Minister, following the election held on 15 October 1964, it was made plain that the abolition of the death penalty was a priority, although it was to be a year before Sidney Silverman introduced another Private Members Bill for the abolition of hanging. The new Home Secretary was himself an abolitionist, and all sentences of death which were delivered between October 1964, when the Labour government took power, and 28 October, when Silverman's Bill received the Royal assent, were commuted.

The last death sentence to be pronounced in England was passed by Mr Justice Havers at Leeds, on 1 November 1965, but both he and David Chapman, the man sentenced to death, knew that he was not going to hang. Although the death penalty for murder was abolished for an initial period of five years, hanging was retained as the punishment for treason, piracy and arson in the Royal Dockyards. The use of the death penalty by military courts, in time of war, was also unaffected by the new law. Five years later, on 16 December 1969, a free vote was held in the commons which endorsed the abolition of hanging for murder. The vote was 343 in favour of abolition and just 185 for retention.

Over the next few years, the other crimes for which death remained the sentence were gradually removed from the statute book. Arson in the Royal Dockyards ceased to be a hanging offence in 1971, with the passage of the Criminal Damage Act 1971. It was rumoured that arson in the dockyards had been added to the Criminal Damage Act due to an upsurge in terrorist activity by the IRA. Since death was the mandatory sentence for this offence, it was conceivable that some terrorist bomber could have ended up facing the death penalty. Even if reprieved, this would generate bad publicity for the British and perhaps provoke a backlash in Northern Ireland. This still left espionage, piracy and treason as capital crimes, as well as a number of purely military offences which could be awarded the death penalty in time of war. In 1957, the Naval Discipline Act limited capital espionage to spying on ships during wartime. The 1981 Armed Forces Act did away with the death penalty for this offence.

Throughout the rest of the twentieth century, the death penalty was still available to the civil courts for treason and piracy, and a court-martial could impose it in wartime for the following crimes:

Serious misconduct in action
Assisting the enemy
Obstructing operations
Giving false air signals
Mutiny and incitement to mutiny
Failure to suppress a mutiny with intent to assist the enemy

All these offences were only punishable by death during time of war.

In 1973, the death penalty was also abolished in Northern Ireland, although it remained technically in force in other parts of the United Kingdom. The last death sentence in Northern Ireland was pronounced in 1973. This was not quite the last death sentence in this country. It is not generally known that the mandatory death penalty for murder was still in force, in parts of Britain, right up to the 1990s. The last death sentence given in the Channel Islands, for instance, was in 1984.

In 1991, Tony Teare was in serious financial difficulties with his bank, who were demanding repayment of an overdraft. Teare contracted himself out as a hired killer, at the extraordinarily cheap rate of £600 a time. His first customer wanted to be rid of a family member called Corrine Bentley. Teare lured her to a remote spot and cut her throat with a Stanley knife. On 10 July 1992, the jury at Douglas Court on the Isle of Man found him guilty of murder, and the judge pronounced sentence. He said:

I can only pronounce one sentence. You will be taken to the Isle of Man jail and thence to a place of legal execution and there hanged by the neck until dead.

This was a legal fiction and, in fact, Tony Teare's sentence was almost immediately commuted to life imprisonment; he was transferred to a prison on the mainland to serve his sentence.

With the abolition of capital punishment, the gallows in 'hanging prisons' were dismantled and the execution suites were used for other purposes. Only one operating gallows remained intact, the one at Wandsworth Prison in south London. Since treason remained on the statute book, and there was the possibility of spies being hanged in some future war, it was thought advisable to keep one gallows in good working order. By 1967, Wandsworth was the only prison in Britain with a gallows.

For the next few years, the gallows was tested regularly in accordance with regulations. By 1973, it was pretty clear that there would not be any more hangings, and the formal testing of the gallows was abandoned. However, the Department for Works still carried out maintenance checks twice a year in June and December. By this time, the condemned cells themselves were being used for other purposes and only the execution chamber remained.

In 1988, the Commons held a free vote on the restoration of capital punishment. Despite the then Prime Minister, Margaret Thatcher, being enthusiastically in favour of hanging, the House voted 341 to 218 against bringing back the death penalty. Another vote, two years later, showed an even greater reluctance to start hanging people again. For the next four years, the gallows at Wandsworth was tested twice a year, even though it was clear that nobody would ever be hanged on it. When, in 1992, plans were made for the complete refurbishment of E Wing (where it was installed), the opportunity was taken quietly to dismantle it and remove it to the Prison Services Museum. That, after all, was what it had become – a museum piece.

A team from the Royal Commission on the Historic Monuments of England visited Wandsworth Prison in January 1993, and staff from the Works Department carried out one final test of the equipment. A heavy bag was placed on the drop with a noose around it and the trapdoors fell. It was the last time that the mechanism was operated, and later that year the gallows were taken to the museum.

The formal and irrevocable end of capital punishment in Britain occurred almost without anybody noticing, shortly before the end of the millennium. The final stages of renouncing, forever, the death penalty in this country both took place in 1998. That year, an amendment was made to the Crime and Disorder Bill which was going through Parliament, to abolish the death penalty for treason and piracy, replacing 'death' with 'life imprisonment'. In May of the same year, Parliament voted to ratify the sixth protocol of the European Convention on Human Rights, which prohibits the use of the death penalty other than in time of war.

After these moves, it was still theoretically possible for a subsequent government to reverse all this, and reinstate hanging. In November 1998, the Human Rights Act 1998 came into force. This absolutely prohibits the use of capital punishment under any circumstances, at any time in the future. As long as Britain remains in the European Union, it is bound by this law.

13

A GALLERY OF BRITISH EXECUTIONERS

Until the nineteenth century and the advent of railway travel, each town and city had its own executioner. During Victoria's reign, hangmen began to move round the country more. Some of the most famous executioners in the last 150 years or so have lived in the north of England, but this did not prevent them from officiating at executions in London, or any other city. We have encountered some executioners by observing their work, but in this chapter I wish to look at their characters; what sort of people chose to pursue this most unsavoury of callings? Before the nineteenth century, relatively little is known about the personalities and private lives of hangmen. For this reason, I propose to skim briefly over the sixteenth, seventeenth and eighteenth centuries, before making a detailed study of some of the most famous executioners from William Calcraft onwards.

The first executioners whose names we know were working in London at the end of the sixteenth century. In France, the Sanson dynasty of executioners lasted for 200 years, with son succeeding father over decades and ultimately centuries. We have had several dynasties of hangmen in this country, although nothing on this scale.

The Brandons

One of the first British executioners, whose name we know, is Gregory Brandon, who was the London hangman in the early seventeenth century. His son Richard took over the role, having worked alongside his father for a while. Richard was known by the crowd as 'Young Gregory', and the gallows was sometimes called the Gregory Tree at that time.

Like a number of executioners, Richard Brandon knew that hanging and beheading people was what he wanted to do when he grew up. As a boy, he used to collect stray cats and dogs from around the neighbourhood, and experiment with the most efficient way of cutting off their heads. This stood him in good stead when, as an adult, he was called upon to cut off the head of the Earl of Strafford, one of Charles I's advisors. There were persistent rumours, a few years later, that it was Richard Brandon who beheaded the King in 1649, although there is no solid evidence for this.

Jack Ketch

In 1663, an executioner was appointed whose name is still remembered, having become synonymous with the hangman over the years. His name is, of course, used for the hangman in the traditional Punch and Judy show. Jack Ketch began working as the London executioner. He had the reputation for being a competent enough hangman, but a bungling headsman. He botched the two most famous beheadings of the late seventeenth century, those of Lord Russell in 1683, and the Duke of Monmouth in 1685. When Lord Russell was sentenced to die, for his supposed part in the Rye House Plot, he accepted the matter stoically, remarking that being beheaded would be no worse than having a tooth pulled. He could not have been more wrong.

On the day of the execution, which took place on the site of the shelter in Lincoln's Inn Fields, near Holborn, Lord Russell tipped the headsman handsomely and laid his head upon the block. Jack Ketch did not remove it with the first stroke of the axe, nor the second. It took three goes to take off the Lord's head, and even the seasoned spectators were disgusted at the inept way that Ketch wielded his axe. He was later moved to write and publish a pamphlet defending his handling of the execution. In the *Apologie*, he justified his bungling by claiming that Lord Russell did not 'dispose himself as was most suitable', and that as a result he had been distracted when swinging the axe down and this had spoiled his aim. Two years later, at the Duke of Monmouth's execution, he took five blows and even then needed to use a butcher's knife to remove the head completely.

John Price (1677-1718)

The eighteenth century saw various hangmen at work, some better than others. It also saw the very beginning of the drop, which would eventually lead to the scientific method of hanging which guaranteed a broken neck, rather than a slow and agonising death from asphyxiation. In 1713, thirty-six-year-old John Price applied for the post of hangman in London. A former sailor and pickpocket, the knowledge of knots that he had gained while working on board ships was to stand him in good stead in his new position. Unfortunately, he had a weakness for drink and it was this that led to his downfall after only a couple of years in the job. He got heavily into debt and was actually escorting a prisoner to an execution at Tyburn, when he was arrested for this. After managing to discharge this debt, he soon found himself in difficulties again and ended up in the Marshalsea debtor's prison, where he spent two years, before escaping in 1718.

Not long after his escape, Price got drunk and raped a woman near Moorfields, a district just outside the city of London. She later died of her injuries and John Price, the hangman, found himself in rather a different role at the next execution he attended. He was hanged at Bunhill Fields, near the site of his crime. The crowd voiced their detestation of this rapist, murderer and one-time executioner in no uncertain manner.

William Marvell

William Marvell, the next hangman in London, also had a weakness for strong liquor and just as in Price's case, this led him into debt. He too was arrested for debt while escorting condemned prisoners to Tyburn. Actually, it is slightly inaccurate to say that he was arrested. The bailiffs attempted to seize him, but the London mob hated bailiffs even more than they did executioners, and a struggle ensued as the crowd freed Marvell from the clutches of those who wished to arrest him. They were so vigorous about this, that Marvell was badly injured, and in no fit state to carry out the triple hanging which was scheduled for that day.

When the cart containing the condemned men arrived, minus the incapacitated hangman, there was a call for a volunteer to take over. One member of the crowd tried to accept the offer, but was promptly beaten up by those around him. In the end, the execution was postponed and the three condemned men were reprieved; their sentences being commuted to transportation to the colonies. This was the fate which eventually befell William Marvell too, when he was later convicted of theft.

John Thrift

Another eighteenth-century hangman worthy of note is John Thrift, who was appointed in 1735. Thrift was a very nervous man, who often seemed to be on the verge of bursting into tears when carrying out his duties. The first execution he conducted at Tyburn was notable for his forgetting to cover the faces of the thirteen men who were hanged. He is remembered as the last executioner in Britain required to remove the heads of living victims, as opposed to the post-mortem butchery practiced upon such men as the Cato Street Conspirators.

On 18 August 1746, the Earl of Kilmarnock and Lord Balmerino, both Jacobite rebels who had taken an active part in the 1745 Scottish uprising, were beheaded on Tower Hill. John Thrift, whose job it was to decapitate the two men, was visibly upset and, in fact, burst into tears when the first of the men, the Earl of Kilmarnock, arrived on the scaffold. This gave rise to the strange situation of the man who was about to die comforting and reassuring the executioner! Thrift managed to behead the Earl with one blow of the axe. Lord Balmerino was even cooler than the Earl of Kilmarnock. He picked up the axe when he had ascended the scaffold and casually ran his finger along the edge. This disconcerted Thrift so badly, that he took three swings to take of the Lord's head. He behaved better at the final judicial beheading of Lord Lovatt, on 9 April 1747. He not only took off Lord Lovatt's head with one stroke, but buried the axe 2in deep in the block while doing so. The block and axe used for this execution are now on display in the Tower of London.

Thomas Turlis

We shall look briefly at one more eighteenth-century hangman, before moving on to the Victorian Era and the men who developed the modern technique of hanging. Thomas Turlis was the hangman for London from 1752 until 1771. One of the most significant hangings which he conducted was that of Lord Ferrers, who murdered his steward. There was a suspicion that Lord Ferrers was mad, but notwithstanding this, he was found guilty of murder. Because the law of England required a man to be tried by his peers, Lord Ferrers had insisted on being tried by the House of Lords. When he had been sentenced to hang for the murder, he petitioned unsuccessfully to have the method of execution changed to beheading.

This execution was one of the first to use a newly-devised mechanical gallows at Tyburn. The traditional method of backing a cart under the triple tree, and then driving off, leaving the condemned men and women swinging on the end of ropes, was starting to look like something of an anachronism. A new gallows had been made in which the victim stood on a platform which would then fall, leaving them suspended after a short drop. Lord Ferrers seemed gratified by the crowds who had come to watch his death. It was not, after all, every day that they saw a Lord hang. The new gallows were not a great success. When the supports to the platform were knocked away, Lord Ferrers fell only a few inches; his toes were actually brushing against the ground. It was necessary for Turlis to hang on his legs in order to finish him off. The execution was also marred by Turlis and his assistant engaging in a fist fight over possession of the hanging rope. Turlis managed to keep it, upon which his assistant started crying. As well he might; the rope used in a famous execution like this could be sold by the inch to souvenir hunters.

William Calcraft (1800-1879)

By the early nineteenth century, hangings were no longer being conducted at Tyburn. Executions were instead held outside Newgate Prison, which stood roughly where the Old Bailey is today. The most famous Victorian hangman, and the first to travel around the country to ply his trade, was William Calcraft. He began working as the London hangman in 1829, but with the advent of the railways, he was called upon to hang people all over the country. He remained in his post for an astonishing forty-five years; by which time he was a doddering old man. A cobbler by trade, as a young man, Calcraft had also sold meat pies at public hangings, where he met John Foxton, one of the hangmen. It is thought that this influenced him to become an executioner himself. Before he started hanging people, Calcraft acquired the job of whipping juvenile offenders, through his connection with Foxton. This was really the job of the hangman himself but served as a kind of apprenticeship for Calcraft.

Calcraft was the last hangman in Britain to be paid a regular wage for the job. So frequent were hangings and floggings, that a full-time man was needed. Later, hangmen were retained on an official list and paid per job, as and when they were needed.

Throughout his professional life, Calcraft favoured the so-called 'short drop'. This method of hanging entailed the victims falling only 18in or 2ft; far enough to stun them, but nowhere near long enough to kill outright, for the most part. This gave him a reputation as something of a callous bungler, which was undeserved. Although it was known that falling with a rope around one's neck could result in death, nobody really understood the mechanics of the thing. Some people might jump from the ladder and still choke to death, while others ended up with broken necks after falling off the cart in the ordinary course of an execution. It was not until the 1870s that it was realised that both the length of the drop, and also the position of the knot, were vital for an effective and humane hanging. A few of Calcraft's victims died of broken necks, but the vast majority did not. In the course of his career, Calcraft hanged over 450 men and women; a record which was to remain unbroken until Albert Pierrepont, a century later.

One of the first hangings undertaken by William Calcraft was that of Thomas Maynard, on 31 December 1829. Maynard's execution was a landmark event, in that it was the last time that anybody in this country was hanged for forgery. It was also Calcraft who carried out the last public execution in Britain, that of Michael Barrett for the Clerkenwell Outrage – an explosion in which twelve people died. The previous year, Calcraft had hanged the three so-called 'Manchester Martyrs' for their part in an attack on a prison van, during which a police officer had been shot dead. This execution had had all the hallmarks of the short drop, with one of the men taking a very long time to die. Things were not improved by Calcraft growing increasingly nervous with advancing age, as the relatives of some of those he had hanged would come after him, seeking revenge. In the case of men like Michael Barrett, and the Manchester Martyrs, this was not an unreasonable fear.

The executions at Manchester took place on 22 November 1867. The entire city was in a state of virtual siege, with a squadron of cavalry deployed near the prison, as well as detachments of highland infantry. There had already been an attempt by Irish nationalists to seize the arsenal at Chester Castle that year, and the authorities were taking no chances with any last minute rescue attempts. William Allen, Michael Larkin and Michael O'Brien were hanged side by side. When the trap fell at eight o'clock that morning, the three men fell from sight, which was just as well. Although Allen died instantly from a broken neck, the other two were still alive. The Catholic priest who was present tells what happened next:

> The other two ropes, stretched taut and tense by their breathing twitch-ing burdens, were in ominous and distracting movement. The hangman had bungled! Calcraft then descended into the pit and there finished what he could not accomplish from above. He killed Larkin.

Calcraft went down into the pit beneath the gallows and swung on William Allen's legs until he was dead. This procedure was his usual way of complet-ing what he had begun, when the rope had failed to do so. The priest, Father Gadd, refused to allow such an undignified death to be inflicted on O'Brien. He remained with the dying man, holding his hands and praying for a hor-rifying three quarters of an hour, until his death.

By all accounts, Calcraft was a phlegmatic and unimaginative man. He seldom spoke of his work and on the rare occasions that he did, showed a lack of feeling bordering on the pathological. Take for example this exchange, when somebody asked Calcraft if he ever became upset at the work he carried out. He was evidently puzzled by the question, 'No, not a bit. Why should I be? I am only doing my job'. The questioner tried again, and asked if having the duty of killing people did not affect him. Calcraft seemed shocked at the very idea, 'Kill a man! Who kills a man? I never killed anybody'. Since this was towards the end of his career, when he had been responsible for hanging over 400 people, there was little that could be said. The old hangman explained how he kept his conscience clear:

> They kills themselves. I merely put the rope round their necks and knock away the platform beneath them. I don't kill them; it's their own weight as does it.

This stupendous piece of sophistry left the person asking the questions speechless, as well it might. William Calcraft was finally pensioned off in 1874.

William Marwood (1820-1883)

The stage was now set for the first truly national hangman, one who did not live in London but whose activities regularly covered the entire country. William Marwood was a fifty-four-year-old cobbler in Lincolnshire. A devout Methodist with an interest in helping his fellow man, he devised in his twenties a scheme whereby the National Debt might be paid off. In later life, he developed a keen interest in hanging, as he felt that the way in which it was being carried out was very cruel. He had a theory that the way to break a neck cleanly, and accurately, every time, involved making a simple calculation based upon the condemned person's weight; the heavier the victim, the shorter the drop, and vice versa. Although he had never even witnessed, much less participated in an execution, he began to write letters to various prisons, offering his services as a hangman. In 1871, the governor of Lincoln Prison invited him to conduct an execution there. His method proved a great success, with the hanged man's neck breaking easily. So impressed were the staff at Lincoln with Marwood's new way of hanging that he began to receive invitations from other prisons. When Calcraft retired in 1874, it was natural that William Marwood would be his successor.

Unlike Calcraft, who was paid a regular salary, William Marwood was only paid per hanging. Despite this, there were a number of advantages to the job, in addition to the fees which he received. For one thing, there was free travel to all the towns where his services were required. His business as a cobbler also became more profitable. A craze started for buying bootlaces from his shop, as grisly souvenirs; people just wanted to be able to say that they had been served by the hangman himself. As a result of this, he hung a sign over his shop saying, 'Crown Officer'. He also raised his prices.

Despite being prepared to profit from his new role, there seems little doubt that Marwood took on the job for humanitarian reasons originally. Unlike Calcraft, very few of his victims died in convulsive agony. He also had a dry sense of humour. While travelling to an execution by train, a fellow passenger declared that he was sure that he had met Marwood before, but was unable to remember when. Marwood replied, 'Well, it wouldn't have been at eight o'clock in the morning'. Marwood was the subject of a popular children's riddle while he was hangman; If Pa killed Ma, who'd kill Pa? Ma would.

Like a number of executioners, William Marwood had a weakness for drink, although it never affected his work. Both Calcraft before him and James Berry who followed were remembered for some ghastly mistakes which led to either strangulation or decapitation, while every execution conducted by Marwood seems to have gone smoothly and painlessly. As he was fond of remarking of his predecessor; 'He hanged them, I execute them'.

Bartholomew Binns (1839-1911)

William Marwood's successor was, to state the case plainly, a drunkard. The night before the first execution which he carried out, on 6 November 1883, he had been showing off the ropes and other equipment in a pub. This execution went well enough, but at the next, things did not go quite as expected. Henry Dutton had been sentenced to death for murdering his wife's grandmother. Nobody knew where Binns had obtained the rope he used for this execution, but one witness described it as being, 'as thick as a ship's hauser'. This meant that the knot could not snap tight, with the result that the wretched Dutton died of asphyxiation and not a broken neck. The doctor who was present at the execution said immediately, 'This is poor work; he is not dead yet.' The victim jerked convulsively for two minutes after the drop.

At the inquest, following Dutton's hanging, the coroner asked pointedly, 'Was the executioner sober?' to which the doctor replied, 'Well, I should not like to say'. It was, by this time, clear to everybody that Binns' appointment had been a terrible mistake. Matters went from bad to worse. In January 1884, Binns was prosecuted for fiddling his fares on the railway. His fares for executions were paid by the county, so presumably he thought that by travelling for nothing, and then claiming his fares anyway, he would make an additional profit on each trip.

Batholomew Binns' final execution was on 10 March 1884. He arrived at the prison drunk and bungled the hanging. He was later criticised for his behaviour, both at the prison and after he had left it. He went straight from the prison to a succession of pubs, where he freely exhibited the ropes and straps which he used in his job. He was removed from the list of officially approved executioners.

James Berry (1852-1913)

James Berry was a Yorkshireman, and his motives in applying for the post of executioner were purely financial. Berry held a succession of low-paid jobs, drifting from working on the railways to becoming, for a time, a police officer, until he finally got a job selling boots. It is an odd coincidence that the three most famous hangmen of the Victorian Era – Calcraft, Marwood and Berry – should all have been involved with boots! He applied for the post of executioner at the same time as Binns, and was bitterly disappointed to be turned down. With the sacking of Binns though, Berry seemed the best candidate of those who had been interviewed the previous year and he was offered the job.

James Berry's first execution was a double one; two poachers had shot dead a couple of gamekeepers who were trying to apprehend them. The execution itself, on 28 March 1884, went smoothly and the two men died without a struggle. It was noticed that Berry's technique differed slightly from that of Marwood. The most efficient method of snapping a person's neck is to place the knot almost under the chin. When the victim is stopped short, after the drop, the head is thrown back sharply and the rope of the noose, the opposite side from the knot, is in direct contact with the back of the neck. This provides the leverage to split apart the vertebrae, breaking the neck and causing instantaneous loss of consciousness. If the knot ends up at the back of the neck, this leverage is not exerted and the result will be strangulation. It was observed that Berry placed the knot under the left ear; the so-called sub-aural position.

It is worth examining James Berry's methods for hanging in detail, because he was later sacked by the Home Office, following a series of unfortunate executions in which at least one of the victims was completely decapitated. He had a predilection for longer drops than his predecessors and this was the most likely cause of these mishaps.

We see in James Berry another of those *leitmotifs* in the history of capital punishment in this country; that is, a hangman with a weakness for drink. It can hardly be a coincidence that so many executioners took to drink in this way. Writing after his retirement from the post, Berry said that he had acquired the habit of:

> Bracing myself up with stimulants. It was an evil I had learned in prison.
> When I went to hang a man, I was never able to do it unless I had had at
> least a gill of brandy.

This habit does not seem to have been noticed when Berry was at work on the scaffold, but in later life he became an alcoholic, attempting suicide at one point.

Although he was the hangman for almost a decade, Berry had a reputation for making mistakes. It was this which finally resulted in his being sacked. One of the most grotesque of his executions and one which did nothing at all for his good reputation, took place on 23 February 1885. It is perhaps unfair to blame Berry for the events of that morning, but it was yet another example of how the executions he conducted seemed to have a habit of going wrong in some way.

John Lee had been convicted of a particularly brutal murder. He had cut the throat of his employer, an elderly woman for whom he was a footman. He claimed to be innocent, but the evidence was overwhelming. His execution was scheduled to take place at Exeter Prison. The gallows was in a shed which doubled as the coach house. Executions were infrequent at Exeter and it had been some time since the gallows had been tested. When he arrived at the prison, the day before the execution was due to take place, Berry checked that the gallows was working. Everything seemed to be in order. Over the weekend there was a good deal of rain and some of it found its way through a leaky roof, making the apparatus of the gallows wet.

At eight o'clock on the morning of Monday 23 February, John Lee was pinioned, brought to the gallows and the noose was placed round his neck. The white hood was drawn over his face and Berry went to the lever to operate it. Nothing happened. He jerked the lever a few times, but the trapdoor refused to open. The bolt had withdrawn and the trapdoors moved a fraction of an inch, but appeared to be jammed. Lee was moved off the trapdoors and Berry tried again, stamping on them and pulling the lever. They opened at once.

It is impossible to imagine the state of mind of the condemned man, having expected to have fallen to his death but still being alive. He was repositioned on the drop and the lever was pulled once again. Once more though, the trapdoors did not open. Lee was removed from the drop and taken to a cell. The gallows were tested again and seemed to be in perfect working order. John Lee was brought back and another attempt was made to hang him. This too failed. Again, he was taken to one side. This time, while he was standing there, prison officers fetched a saw and various pieces of wood were removed from the trapdoors. All this was too much for both the chaplain and the doctor, who both refused to participate any further in the business. Without their presence, the execution could not take place and later that day, Lee was reprieved and his sentence commuted to life imprisonment.

The most likely explanation for the failure of the gallows was that the leaves of the trapdoor had become swollen by the rain, which had trickled onto them. The weight of the condemned man standing on them was enough to cause them to jam tight. None of this was really Berry's fault, but three months later, he almost managed to pull off Moses Shrimpton's head while hanging him. On this occasion, the pit below the gallows was awash with blood and the dead man's head was only hanging on by a few shreds of muscle. Later that year, he managed to pull off Robert Goodale's head completely; this gave the impression of a man who was having difficulty in hanging his victims efficiently.

Another cause for concern was James Berry's conduct. Like Binns, he began hanging around in pubs on the night before executions. This happened prior to one of Berry's last executions, which went terribly wrong. The condemned man was John Conway, and he had been sentenced to death for the murder of a child. He was hanged on 20 August 1891.

Berry claimed later that he had not been allowed to give Conway the length of drop that he would have chosen. Whatever the facts of the case, the end result was appalling. At this time, newspaper reporters were permitted as witnesses to hangings and so we have several independent accounts of what happened that morning. After the drop fell, the sound of running liquid was audible to everybody. One witness described it as being like the sound of a fountain. The reporters rushed to look into the pit beneath the gallows at once. But they soon wished that they had not done so, because the place was covered with blood. Conway's head had all but been ripped off and was only attached to his body by a few pieces of skin and flesh. In October 1891, the Home Office made it clear that Berry should never again be engaged as a hangman.

The Billingtons

James Billington (1847-1901)

Two families dominate the story of hanging between 1884 and its abolition in 1964. One of these is fairly well know; most people have heard vaguely of the Pierrepoints. Few are familiar with the Billingtons. James Billington had applied to be the hangman for London in 1884, at the same time as James Berry. A Yorkshireman like Berry, he had been turned down for this coveted role and had to content himself with being appointed the executioner for Yorkshire. As soon as Berry's services were dispensed with in 1891, Billington knew that his time had come. There had been a certain amount of rivalry between the two men, with Billington undertaking a number of executions in Yorkshire, the very country in which James Berry also lived.

Like a number of other famous hangmen, James Billington had a lifelong interest in the subject of execution. He first applied to be a hangman at the same time as Marwood. He was only twenty-five at the time, and it was to be another twelve years before he achieved his ambition. He ran a barber's shop when he was not engaged in hanging people and was a popular and cheerful man. Three of his sons followed him into the trade. Thomas and William both assisted their father at executions and following his death, William inherited his post as principle executioner for the country. He enlisted the help of his brother John, who in turn became an executioner in his own right. For over thirty years, Billington and sons were carrying out executions in this country. John Billington died at the very young age of twenty-five as a result of an accident at work. While preparing the gallows before an execution, he fell into the pit, cracking his ribs badly. This led to pleurisy, of which he died.

The Pierrepoints

Henry Pierrepoint (1878-1922)

Henry Pierrepoint was born into a working-class family in Nottingham. The family moved to Bradford while he was young and this is where he grew up. From his childhood, Henry Pierrepoint's ambition was to be an executioner. He followed the accounts of murders and hangings in the newspapers and was captivated by the exciting life and interesting experiences of James Billington, who, like Henry, lived in Yorkshire. In February 1901, a few weeks before his twenty-third birthday, by which time he was living in Manchester, Pierrepoint wrote directly to the Home Secretary, offering his services as a hangman. Perhaps the Home Secretary was flattered to be approached in this way. At any rate, he wrote to the governor of Strangeways Prison in Manchester, suggesting that he interview this young man to assess his suitability to become an executioner.

Incredibly, within a few months, Henry Pierrepoint found himself on the official list of those approved to assist in executions. It was not until November of that year that his services were called upon; he was to act as assistant to James Billington at a hanging in Newgate Prison. The event passed off without incident. The next month, he was again invited to assist James Billington, this time at an execution in Manchester itself. The condemned man was known to Billington, who was depressed about the prospect of hanging a friend. Nevertheless, he went through with it. It was the last execution he would ever perform. A fortnight later, he died of pneumonia and the following month, Henry Pierrepoint found himself unexpectedly promoted to being a hangman, authorised to carry out executions as chief executioner. It had taken him less than a year to fulfil his childhood ambition.

Henry Pierrepoint went on to hang over 100 people, often working with one or other of James Billington's sons. There was, at this time, a shortage of assistant executioners. This prompted Henry Pierrepoint to suggest that his brother Thomas apply to become a hangman. He did so and the two brothers worked amicably together for some years. In 1905, Henry's wife gave birth to a son, whom they christened Albert. He was of course to become the most prolific hangman of the twentieth century.

At the first hanging which Henry Pierrepoint conducted as principle executioner, he was assisted by a man called John Ellis. We shall be reading about him shortly, but for now it is enough to say that a rivalry grew between these two men. In later years, Henry Pierrepoint became convinced that Ellis was trying to supplant him. As we shall see, that is precisely what happened in the end, but whether this was the culmination of some cunning plan which John Ellis had nurtured for years or whether it was caused by Henry Pierrepoint's own conduct is a moot point.

Henry Pierrepoint's downfall was caused by the same problem which had bedevilled many hangmen over the centuries; that is to say drink. The Aberdare Committee's rules about hangmen arriving at the prison on the afternoon before an execution had been designed to prevent alcohol being consumed on the night before a hanging, or on the morning of the execution itself. Of course, this could not prevent a hangman from spending the day in the pub before he even got to the prison. This is exactly what Henry Pierrepoint did on 13 July 1910.

Pierrepoint arrived at Chelmsford Prison just before four o'clock on 13 July, in order to hang Frederick Foreman the following day. He found John Ellis, his assistant, already there. It was obvious to everybody that Henry Pierrepoint was drunk. He was affable enough at first, but then became quarrelsome. Taking offence at some fancied slight, he launched a furious attack on Ellis, knocking him down. Although the execution the next morning went smoothly and Pierrepoint and Ellis seemed to have patched up their differences, this affair had a disastrous effect upon Henry Pierrepoint's career. Ellis wrote to the Home Office complaining about his treatment at Pierrepoint's hands, and following discreet enquiries of the staff at Chelmsford Prison, a memo was circulated forbidding any further use of Henry Pierrepoint as a hangman.

The loss of income from his part-time job as hangman was a serious blow for Henry Pierrepoint. He was never officially notified of his removal from the approved list of executioners; it was simply that his brother Tom and John Ellis received all the invitations from prisons, while he himself had none.

After almost a year of being cold shouldered in this way, Pierrepoint wrote to the Home Office. He asked whether or not he would still be used as a hangman in the future, explaining that, 'I have a wife and five children to keep and I can assure you that I have had a lot to bear.' It was to no avail; he was never again to participate in an execution. John Ellis came to rank equally with Tom Pierrepoint as a chief executioner.

Tom Pierrepoint (1870-1954)

Tom Pierrepoint had been encouraged to become first his assistant, and later an executioner in his own right, by his brother Henry. His career was an extremely long one, almost rivalling that of William Calcraft. He carried out his last execution at the astonishingly advanced age of seventy-six; executing almost 300 people in the course of his work as an executioner.

To begin with, Tom worked for some years as his brother's assistant. The two men understood each other and made a good team, working instinctively. There were still occasional problems during executions, although these were not caused by any shortcomings on the part of the Pierrepoint brothers. An incidence of this took place when Tom and Henry were hanging a man in Ireland. In January 1910, the brothers took a ferry to Ireland, to execute a man called Richard Heffernan.

When they arrived at Kilmainham Prison in Dublin, they discovered that there was a good deal of anxiety about the execution which was to be carried out. The condemned man was young, healthy and strong and had already made two attempts at suicide since his trial. On one occasion, he had tried to tear out his own throat with his bare hands, and on another had dived head first at a wall, fracturing his skull. He had also attacked prison guards on two separate occasions. So distressed was his state, that he had been kept sedated in the prison hospital. Now that his execution was imminent, he had been returned to the condemned cell.

Henry Pierrepoint had a presentiment that the execution would not go smoothly, and he warned his brother about this as they prepared for bed that night. Although the English executioners were very impressed with Kilmainham Prison – it was extremely well-kept and the scaffold and gallows were in excellent order – there was a difficulty with the execution chamber itself. It was a cramped room, with almost all the available floor space being taken up by the trapdoors of the gallows. There was a space of barely 18in around the room for all the witnesses and officials to stand, and this did not give much room for the hangman to work. This room was at the end of a narrow corridor leading from the condemned cell.

As the clock struck eight o'clock the next morning, Henry and Tom Pierrepoint entered the cell. To their surprise, they found not one, but two priests ministering to Heffernan. One was holding a large crucifix for the condemned man to kiss, while the other was reciting prayers. Heffernan himself was in a hysterically distressed state, sobbing and crying with fear. The Pierrepoints did not like to interrupt the religious devotions, but since these showed no signs of abating, they felt that they had to get on with the job. Fastening their victim's hands behind his back, the party set off along the corridor to the gallows.

Because the corridor was so narrow, and due to the fact that there were two priests instead of the usual one, the procession to the gallows developed into something of a rugby scrum, rather than a solemn and dignified walk. The priests were still clustered round the condemned man, who was stumbling forward in a daze. When they reached the execution chamber, the various officials positioned themselves around the narrow edge of the trapdoors. Tom Pierrepoint pinioned Heffernan's legs, while his brother placed the noose around their victim's neck, whilst pulling the white hood over his face. The two executioners then darted off the drop. Henry Pierrepoint was just about to pull the lever, when he noticed to his horror that the priests were still hugging and consoling Heffernan. Heffernan himself was swaying and was obviously on the verge of collapsing. Henry rushed onto the drop and pushed the priests out of the way roughly, and then got his brother to stand next to the fainting man to support him. As soon as everything was ready, Tom darted off the trapdoors and Henry pulled the lever. It was one of the worst executions that either man had experienced.

Throughout the 1920s, Tom Pierrepoint was hanging a dozen men a year. One of the men he executed during this period was notable for having been sentenced to death twice, on the same day. Samuel Cushnan, a farm labourer, had shot dead a postman in Belfast. The motive for the crime was to steal postal orders from the mailbag. On 9 March 1930, Cushnan was found guilty and sentenced to be hanged on 8 April 1929. He had been removed from the dock before this mistake was noticed, and had to be brought back so that he could be sentenced to hang in 1930, instead of the previous year. He appealed against his sentence on the grounds of the mental anguish which this had caused him to suffer. But on 8 April 1930, Tom Pierrepoint hanged him in Crumlin Road Prison.

At about this time, Pierrepoint received a letter from the Home Office, reminding him that he should not be touting for work. The following year, Tom Pierrepoint's twenty-six-year-old nephew Albert, Henry Pierrepoint's son, applied to become an assistant executioner. Albert Pierrepoint would become the most prolific hangman in British, and possibly world history.

As the years passed and Tom Pierrepoint showed no sign of resigning, some prison staff began to express their doubts about the wisdom of engaging a man in his seventies to undertake executions. At the execution of forty-two-year-old Herbert Bounds, in November 1942, the governor of Wandsworth Prison was so concerned about Pierrepoint's conduct that he wrote to the Prison Commission about the matter. The main complaint was that Pierrepoint had interrupted the spiritual consolation which the condemned man had been receiving, and hustled him to the scaffold with more haste than was strictly necessary. The governor said in his letter:

> If the Minister's influence over the prisoner is brought to a close too abruptly, a more unhappy scene is witnessed that, in my opinion is necessary.
>
> I formed the opinion that Mr Pierrepoint at his advanced age, I believe his age is 72 years – has passed his peak of efficiency and is becoming less tactful and more abrupt in his methods. It impressed me as though he had turned what I would call an unpleasant episode of drastic efficiency, into a more unpleasant one.

This was not the first time that attention had been drawn to Tom Pierrepoint's age. He was certainly brusque with clergymen who got in the way during an execution, perhaps remembering the unfortunate scene in Dublin many years earlier.

The following year, the governor of Wandsworth again wrote to the Prison Commissioners. They replied fairly curtly, saying:

> Owing to wartime difficulties of replacements and favourable reports from other prisons, the Commissioners are inclined to allow Mr Pierrepoint to act.

In other words, the message was plain, 'Don't you know there's a war on? Stop being such a fusspot!' Once the war ended though, the invitations dried up for Tom Pierrepoint, and his nephew took over for the next decade as chief hangman.

Albert Pierrepoint (1905-1992)

When Albert Pierrepoint was eleven, he was asked at school to write a composition with the title 'What I would like to be when I grow up'. The rest of the class wanted to be engine drivers and explorers; Albert's ambition was to be a hangman. Still, with a father and uncle who were executioners, perhaps we cannot really blame the Yorkshire schoolboy. He certainly fulfilled his childhood ambition, growing up to hang over 400 men and women.

Albert Pierrepoint applied to become an executioner in 1931, when he was just twenty-six. Coming from such a family, it was more or less a formality and the following year he first assisted his uncle at a hanging. It was to be another nine years before he was invited to act as hangman himself. This was the execution of a gangland murderer called Mancini, in 1941. According to Pierrepoint's autobiography, written in the 1970s, the prison governor sent for him after this first execution and told him:

I have seen your uncle work on many occasions. He is a very good man indeed. Never has he been any quicker than you have been this morning.

Albert went on to hang another thirty people during the course of the Second World War. It was after the end of the war that his career as executioner really took off. The decision had been made that the Americans would undertake the execution of senior Nazi leaders following the trials at Nuremburg. All the evidence suggests that these hangings were badly botched. The Americans were still using a short drop and the old style 'cowboy coil' noose. Some of the men choked to death, while others had their faces damaged by the trapdoors as they fell to their deaths.

The British decided that Albert Pierrepoint would carry out the hanging of convicted war criminals in their own sector. In the three years from the end of 1945 to late 1948, he executed 200 Nazis found guilty of war crimes. He flew to Germany to undertake this work, the majority of which was done at Hameln. Pierrepoint hanged many high-profile figures, including the former Commandant of Belsen concentration camp and Irma Grese; the so-called 'blond beast'.

From the end of the war until 1956, Albert Pierrepoint was the chief executioner in this country. He hanged most of the famous murderers of this period; men such as Haigh, Christie and Derek Bentley. On 17 June 1954, he carried out the last double execution to take place in this country. The two men, who were hanged together at Pentonville, died for a completely pointless crime. Ian Grant and Kenneth Gilbert, both aged twenty-one, had been robbing a hotel of cigarettes and were disturbed by the night porter. They tied him up and gagged him, causing him to choke to death. Their execution went off without a hitch.

The circumstances surrounding Albert Pierrepoint's retirement have always been a little mysterious. On 13 July 1955, he hanged Ruth Ellis, the last woman to be executed in this country. After this, he carried out two more executions and then stopped abruptly. The rumour, popular at the time, was that the hanging of Ruth Ellis had affected Pierrepoint badly. He always denied this. It must be remembered that John Ellis, the man who hanged Edith Thompson in 1922, also resigned suddenly a year or two after executing a woman. In Ellis' case, the event so traumatised him, that he attempt suicide twice, being successful on the second attempt. Could the same feelings of revulsion for executing a woman have been at work in Albert Pierrepoint?

A more prosaic explanation for his sudden and unexpected resignation emerged after Albert Pierrepoint's death. He had been asked to carry out a double execution at Strangeways Prison in Manchester on 3 January 1956. This promised to be quite profitable, netting him £25; equivalent to perhaps £400 or £500 at today's value. Three days before the execution, one of the two men was reprieved. This left a man called Thomas Bancroft to face the hangman alone.

On 2 January, Pierrepoint and his assistant, Harry Allen, arrived at the prison and began preparations for the hanging. At eight o'clock that evening, while they were having their evening meal, the governor sent word that a reprieve had been received. This was the latest reprieve to be granted in the twentieth century; Thomas Bancroft came within twelve hours of being hanged. Because he had travelled all the way to the prison, and spent the night in Manchester, Pierrepoint felt that he should be entitled to the full fee for the execution. He had taken time from his job and lost as much time as he would have done had he actually carried out the hanging. The Under-Sheriff for the area though, took the view that it was unreasonable of Pierrepoint to expect to be paid for a job which he had not carried out.

Three weeks later, Albert Pierrepoint wrote to the Prison Commissioners:

Dear Sir,
I was engaged by the Under-Sheriff of Lancashire to carry out an execution of T. Bancroft at HM Prison Manchester on the 3rd of January last. I reported for duty in the usual way. Later in the evening I was informed by the governor that Bancroft had been respited.

I left the prison at about 8.30 p.m. and as it was a very bad evening I had to stay overnight in Manchester, also on leaving work I had to engage extra staff to look after my business in my absence. On returning home I was only paid my out of pocket travelling expenses.

The Under-Sheriff informs me that he has no ruling in this matter of paying fees in this particular case. I feel sure that after making all necessary arrangements and reporting for duty I was entitled to my full fees, which has been granted to me on other occasions.

I would be much obliged if you would give me a ruling on this matter.
I am your obedient servant,
A. Pierrepoint

A reply was sent to Pierrepoint, reminding him of the terms to which he agreed when he first became an assistant executioner back in 1932. This was that if a reprieve was granted, the hangman received no fee. He brooded on this for a fortnight, before writing back:

Dear Sir,

I beg to acknowledge the receipt of your letter of the 8th instant.

From the Under-Sheriff of Lancashire I have received a cheque for £4 which apparently was regarded as an adequate recompense for my attendance at HM Prison Manchester, concerning a contract in which a reprieve was granted.

I must inform you that I was extremely dissatisfied with this payment, and now I regard this kind of meanness as surprising in view of my experience and long service.

In the circumstances I have made up my mind to resign and this letter must be accepted as a letter of resignation. I request the removal of my name from the list of executioners forthwith.

Yours faithfully,

A. Pierrepoint

Harry Allen (1911-1992)

Following Albert Pierrepoint's unexpected resignation in 1955, two men were jointly promoted to the post of chief executioner. One was Harry Allen and the other Robert Leslie Stewart. Harry Allen had first applied to become an assistant executioner in the 1930s, but had been turned down by the Home Office, possibly because of his youth. He applied again a few years later and was accepted for training. After assisting both Tom and Albert Pierrepoint at executions, Harry Allen became an executioner himself, carrying out both the last hanging in Northern Ireland in 1961, as well as the last Scottish execution in Aberdeen on 15 August 1963. In total, he hanged twenty-nine men. His career as an executioner came to an end in 1964, when he hanged Gwynne Owen Evans at Strangeways Prison in Manchester. This was one of the final executions in Britain.

Harry Allen took great pride in his work, and always dressed very smartly when carrying out his official duties. A peculiarity of his was that he always wore a bow tie when hanging people.

Robert Leslie Stewart (1918-1989)

One of the last hangmen in this country, Robert Leslie Stewart, began assist-ing at executions during the 1950s. He assisted at twenty-nine hangings and carried out seven as chief executioner. On 13 August 1964, he hanged Peter Anthony Allen at Walton Prison in Liverpool. This execution took place at the same time as that of Peter Allen's accomplice in Manchester. These were the last executions to take place in the United Kingdom. Six years earlier, in May 1958, Stewart had carried out the last execution in Wales.

BIBLIOGRAPHY

Abbott, G., *Lipstick on the Noose* (Summersdale Publishers, 2003)

Brandon, D., & Brooke, A., *London: The Executioner's City* (Sutton Publishing, 2006)

Clarke, P., Hardy, L., & Williams, A., *Executioners* (Futura, 2008)

Clark, R., *Women and the Noose* (Tempus, 2007)

Corns, C. & Hughes-Wilson, J., *Blindfold and Alone* (Cassell, 2001)

Evans, S., *Executioner* (Sutton Publishing, 2004)

Fielding, S., *Pierrepoint: A Family of Executioners* (John Blake Publishing, 2006)

Fielding, S., *The Executioner's Bible* (John Blake Publishing, 2008)

Green, J., *Famous Last Words* (Omnibus Press, 1979)

Homer, T., *The Book of Origins* (Piatkus Books, 2006)

Innes, B., *The History of Torture* (Brown Packaging, 1998)

Knipe, W., *Tyburn Tales* (The History Press, 2010)

McLaughlin, S., *Execution Suite: A History of the Gallows at Wandsworth Prison 1878-1993* (Wandsworth Prison Museum, 2004)

Pierrepoint, A., *Executioner: Pierrepoint* (Harrap, 1974)

Seddon, P., *Laws Strangest Cases* (Anova Books, 2005)

Slee, C., *The Guinness Book of Lasts* (Guinness World Records Ltd, 1994)

Tibballs, G., *Legal Blunders* (Robinson, 2000)

Other titles published by The History Press

Prisons & Prisoners in Victorian Britain

NEIL R. STOREY

Featuring stories of crime and misdeeds, this book includes chapters on a typical day inside a Victorian prison, including food, divine service, exercise and medical provision; the punishments inflicted on convicts – such as hard labour, flogging, the treadwheel and shot drill; and an overview of the ultimate penalty paid by prisoners – execution. Richly illustrated with a series of photographs, engravings, documents and letters, this volume is sure to appeal to all those interested in true crime and social history in Victorian Britain.

978 0 7524 5269 2

Hanged at Gloucester

JILL EVANS

This book gathers together the stories of the 123 prisoners who were executed at Gloucester between 1792 and 1939, when the last convict was executed within the prison's walls. Infamous cases include the Berkeley poachers, who shot and killed the Earl of Berkeley's gamekeeper; Rebecca Worlock, who poisoned her husband with arsenic; notorious robbers Matthew and Henry Pinnell; and Charlotte Long, the last woman to be hanged for arson in England.

978 0 7524 5818 2

Murder & Crime: Whitechapel & District

MARK RIPPER

Jack the Ripper's brutal murders have left an ineradicable stain on the streets of Whitechapel. Disturbingly, his infamous butchery was just one of many equally deplorable atrocities committed in London's East End. Cases featured here include that of Henry Wainwright, tried in 1875 for the murder and dismemberment of his mistress; Israel Lipski, charged with the murder of a fellow lodger in 1887; and Myer Abramovitch, executed in 1912 for double murder.

978 0 7524 5549 5

Devon Villains: Rogues, Rascals & Reprobates

MIKE HOLGATE

Read about legendary north Devon highwayman Tom Faggus, east Devon smuggler Jack Rattenbury, south Devon murderer John Lee ('The Man They Could Not Hang') and west Devon fraudster Charles De Ville Wells , as well as many other infamous rogues, rascals and reprobates in this veritable who's who of the county's most notorious villains.

978 0 7524 6074 1

Visit our website and discover thousands of other History Press books.

www.thehistorypress.co.uk